SUMMER AND SMOKE

SUMMER and SMOKE

By TENNESSEE WILLIAMS

Who, if I were to cry out, would hear me among the angelic orders?

Rilke

A NEW DIRECTIONS BOOK

MANUFACTURED IN THE U.S.A.

CHARACTERS

ALMA as a child

JOHN as a child

REV. WINEMILLER, her father

MRS. WINEMILLER, her mother

ALMA WINEMILLER

JOHN BUCHANAN, JR.

DR. BUCHANAN, his father

ROSA GONZALES

PAPA GONZALES, her father

NELLIE EWELL

MRS. BASSETT

ROGER DOREMUS

MR. KRAMER

ROSEMARY

VERNON

DUSTY

SCENES

A SUMMER

PROLOGUE: The Fountain
SCENE 1   The same
SCENE 2   The Rectory Interior & Doctor's Office
SCENE 3   The Rectory Interior
SCENE 4   The Doctor's Office
SCENE 5   The Rectory Interior
SCENE 6   The Arbor

PART TWO

A WINTER

SCENE 7   The Rectory & Doctor's Office
SCENE 8   The Doctor's Office
SCENE 9   The Rectory & Doctor's Office
SCENE 10   The Fountain
SCENE 11   The Doctor's Office
SCENE 12   The Fountain

The entire action of the play takes place in Glorious Hill, Mississippi. The time is the turn of the Century through 1916.

AUTHOR'S PRODUCTION NOTES

As the concept of a design grows out of reading a play I will not do more than indicate what I think are the most essential points.

First of all—*The Sky*.

There must be a great expanse of sky so that the entire action of the play takes place against it. This is true of interior as well as exterior scenes. But in fact there are no really interior scenes, for the walls are omitted or just barely suggested by certain necessary fragments such as might be needed to hang a picture or to contain a door-frame.

During the day scenes the sky should be a pure and intense blue (like the sky of Italy as it is so faithfully represented in the religious paintings of the Renaissance) and costumes should be selected to form dramatic color contrasts to this intense blue which the figures stand against. (Color harmonies and other visual effects are tremendously important.)

In the night scenes, the more familiar constellations, such as Orion and the Great Bear and the Pleiades, are clearly projected on the night sky, and above them, splashed across the top of the cyclorama, is the nebulous radiance of the Milky Way. Fleecy cloud forms may also be projected on this cyclorama and made to drift across it.

So much for *The Sky*.

Now we descend to the so-called interior sets of the play. There are two of these "interior" sets, one being the parlor of an Episcopal Rectory and the other the home of a doctor next door to the Rectory. The architecture of these houses is barely suggested but is of an American Gothic design of the Victorian era. There are no actual doors or windows or walls. Doors and windows are represented by delicate frameworks of Gothic design. These frames have strings of ivy clinging to them, the leaves of emerald and amber. Sections of wall are used only where they are functionally required. There should be a fragment of wall in back of the Rectory sofa, supporting a romantic landscape in a gilt frame. In the doctor's house there should be a section of wall to support the chart of anatomy. Chirico has used fragmentary walls and interiors in a very evocative way in his painting called "Conversation among the Ruins." We will deal more specifically with these interiors as we come to them in the course of the play.

Now we come to the main exterior set which is a promontory in a park or public square in the town of Glorious Hill. Situated on this promontory is a fountain in the form of a stone angel, in a gracefully crouching position with wings lifted and her hands held together to form a cup from which water flows, a public drinking fountain. The stone angel of the fountain should probably be elevated so that it appears in the background of the interior scenes as a symbolic figure (Eternity) brooding over the course of the play. *This entire exterior set may be on an upper level, above that of the two fragmentary interiors.* I would like all three units to form an harmonious whole like one complete picture rather than three separate ones. An imaginative designer may solve these plastic problems in a variety of ways and should not feel bound by any of my specific suggestions.

There is one more set, a very small exterior representing an arbor, which we will describe when we reach it.

Everything possible should be done to give an unbroken fluid quality to the sequence of scenes.

There should be no curtain except for the intermission. The other divisions of the play should be accomplished by changes of lighting.

Finally, the matter of music. One basic theme should recur and the points of recurrence have been indicated here and there in the stage directions.

Rome, March, 1948.

Summer and Smoke was first produced by Margo Jones at her theater in Dallas, Texas. It was later produced and directed by Miss Jones in New York, opening at the Music Box Theater, October 6, 1948, with Margaret Phillips and Tod Andrews in the two leading roles; incidental music by Paul Bowles and setting by Jo Mielziner.

CAST OF THE NEW YORK PRODUCTION

ALMA as a child	ARLENE McQUADE
JOHN as a child	DONALD HASTINGS
REV. WINEMILLER	RAYMOND VAN SICKLE
MRS. WINEMILLER	MARGA ANN DEIGHTON
ALMA WINEMILLER	MARGARET PHILLIPS
JOHN BUCHANAN, Jr.	TOD ANDREWS
DR. BUCHANAN	RALPH THEADORE
ROSA GONZALES	MONICA BOYAR
PAPA GONZALES	SID CASSEL
NELLIE EWELL	ANNE JACKSON
MRS. BASSETT	BETTY GREENE LITTLE
ROGER DOREMUS	EARL MONTGOMERY
MR. KRAMER	RAY WALSTON
ROSEMARY	ELLEN JAMES
VERNON	SPENCER JAMES
DUSTY	WILLIAM LAYTON
A GIRL	HILDY PARKS

PART ONE

A SUMMER

KERR

Alma Winemiller—the tragic, idealistic and repressed small town girl of Glorious Hill, Mississippi.

PROLOGUE

In the park near the angel of the fountain. At dusk of an evening in May, in the first few years of this Century.

Alma, as a child of ten, comes into the scene. She wears a middy blouse and has ribboned braids. She already has the dignity of an adult; there is a quality of extraordinary delicacy and tenderness or spirituality in her, which must set her distinctly apart from other children. She has a habit of holding her hands, one cupped under the other in a way similar to that of receiving the wafer at Holy Communion. This is a habit that will remain with her as an adult. She stands like that in front of the stone angel for a few moments; then bends to drink at the fountain.

While she is bent at the fountain, John, as a child, enters. He shoots a pea-shooter at Alma's bent-over back. She utters a startled cry and whirls about. He laughs.

JOHN:
Hi, Preacher's daughter. [*He advances toward her.*] I been looking for you.

ALMA [*hopefully*]:
You have?

JOHN:
Was it you that put them handkerchiefs on my desk? [*Alma smiles uncertainly.*] Answer up!

ALMA:
I put a box of handkerchiefs on your desk.

JOHN:
I figured it was you. What was the idea, Miss Priss?

ALMA:
You needed them.

1

JOHN:
Trying to make a fool of me?

ALMA:
Oh, no!

JOHN:
Then what was the idea?

ALMA:
You have a bad cold and your nose has been running all week. It spoils your appearance.

JOHN:
You don't have to look at me if you don't like my appearance.

ALMA:
I like your appearance.

JOHN [*coming closer*]:
Is that why you look at me all the time?

ALMA:
I—don't!

JOHN:
Oh, yeh, you do. You been keeping your eyes on me all the time. Every time I look around I see them cat eyes of yours looking at me. That was the trouble today when Miss Blanchard asked you where the river Amazon was. She asked you twice and you still didn't answer because you w' lookin' at me. What's the idea? What've'y' got on y' mind anyhow? Answer up!

ALMA:
I was only thinking how handsome you'd be if your face wasn't dirty. You know why your face is dirty? Because you don't use a handkerchief and you wipe your nose on the sleeve of that dirty old sweater.

2

JOHN [*indignantly*]:
Hah!

ALMA:
That's why I put the handkerchiefs on your desk and I
wrapped them up so nobody would know what they were.
It isn't my fault that you opened the box in front of everybody!

JOHN:
What did you think I'd do with a strange box on my desk?
Just leave it there till it exploded or something? Sure I
opened it up. I didn't expect to find no—*handkerchiefs!*—
in it . . .

ALMA [*in a shy trembling voice*]:
I'm sorry that you were embarrassed. I honestly am awfully
sorry that you were embarrassed. Because I wouldn't embarrass you for the world!

JOHN:
Don't flatter yourself that I was embarrassed. I don't embarrass that easy.

ALMA:
It was stupid and cruel of those girls to laugh.

JOHN:
Hah!

ALMA:
They should all realize that you don't have a mother to take
care of such things for you. It was a pleasure to me to be
able to do something for you, only I didn't want you to
know it was me who did it.

JOHN:
Hee-haw! Ho-hum! Take 'em back! [*He snatches out the
box and thrusts it toward her.*]

ALMA:

Please keep them.

JOHN:

What do I want with them?

[*She stares at him helplessly. He tosses the box to the ground and goes up to the fountain and drinks. Something in her face mollifies him and he sits down at the base of the fountain with a manner that does not preclude a more friendly relation. The dusk gathers deeper.*]

ALMA:

Do you know the name of the angel?

JOHN:

Does she have a name?

ALMA:

Yes, I found out she does. It's carved in the base, but it's all worn away so you can't make it out with your eyes.

JOHN:

Then how do you know it?

ALMA:

You have to read it with your fingers. I did and it gave me cold shivers! *You* read it and see if it doesn't give *you* cold shivers! Go on! Read it with your fingers!

JOHN:

Why don't you tell me and save me the trouble?

ALMA:

I'm not going to tell you.

[*John grins indulgently and turns to the pediment, crouching before it and running his fingers along the worn inscription.*]

JOHN:
E?

ALMA:
Yes, E is the first letter!

JOHN:
T?

ALMA:
Yes!

JOHN:
E?

ALMA:
E!

JOHN:
K?

ALMA:
No, no, not K!—R! [*He slowly straightens up.*]

JOHN:
Eternity?

ALMA:
Eternity!—Didn't it give you the cold shivers?

JOHN:
Nahh.

ALMA:
Well, it did me!

JOHN:
Because you're a preacher's daughter. Eternity. What is eternity?

ALMA [*in a hushed wondering voice*]:
It's something that goes on and on when life and death and time and everything else is all through with.

JOHN:

There's no such thing.

ALMA:

There is. It's what people's souls live in when they have left their bodies. My name is Alma and Alma is Spanish for soul. Did you know that?

JOHN:

Hee-haw! Ho-hum! Have you ever seen a dead person?

ALMA:

No.

JOHN:

I have. They made me go in the room when my mother was dying and she caught hold of my hand and wouldn't let me go—and so I screamed and hit her.

ALMA:

Oh, you didn't do that.

JOHN [*somberly*]:

Uh-huh. She didn't look like my mother. Her face was all ugly and yellow and—terrible—bad-smelling! And so I hit her to make her let go of my hand. They told me that I was a devil!

ALMA:

You didn't know what you were doing.

JOHN:

My dad is a doctor.

ALMA:

I know.

JOHN:

He wants to send me to college to study to be a doctor but I wouldn't be a doctor for the world. And have to go in a room and watch people dying! . . . Jesus!

ALMA:

You'll change your mind about that.

JOHN:

Oh, no, I won't. I'd rather *be* a devil, like they called me and go to South America on a boat! . . . Give me one of them handkerchiefs. [*She brings them eagerly and humbly to the fountain. He takes one out and wets it at the fountain and scrubs his face with it.*] Is my face clean enough to suit you now?

ALMA:

Yes!—Beautiful!

JOHN:

What!

ALMA:

I said "Beautiful"!

JOHN:

Well—let's—kiss each other.

[*Alma turns away.*]

JOHN:

Come on, let's just try it!

[*He seizes her shoulders and gives her a quick rough kiss. She stands amazed with one hand cupping the other.*

[*The voice of a child in the distance calls "Johnny! Johnny!"*

[*He suddenly snatches at her hair-ribbon, jerks it loose and then runs off with a mocking laugh.*

[*Hurt and bewildered, Alma turns back to the stone angel, for comfort. She crouches at the pediment and touches the inscription with her fingers. The scene dims out with music.*]

7

SCENE ONE

Before the curtain rises a band is heard playing a patriotic anthem, punctuated with the crackle of fireworks.

The scene is the same as for the Prologue. It is the evening of July 4th in a year shortly before the first World War. There is a band concert and a display of fireworks in the park. During the scene the light changes from faded sunlight to dusk. Sections of roof, steeples, weather-vanes, should have a metallic surface that catches the mellow light on the backdrop; when dusk has fallen the stars should be visible.

As the curtain rises, the Rev. and Mrs. Winemiller come in and sit on the bench near the fountain. Mrs. Winemiller was a spoiled and selfish girl who evaded the responsibilities of later life by slipping into a state of perverse childishness. She is known as Mr. Winemiller's "Cross."

MR. WINEMILLER [*suddenly rising*]:
There is Alma, getting on the bandstand! [*Mrs. Winemiller is dreamily munching popcorn.*]

AN ANNOUNCER'S VOICE [*at a distance*]:
The Glorious Hill Orchestra brings you Miss Alma Winemiller, The Nightingale of the Delta, singing . . . "La Golondrina."

MR. WINEMILLER [*sitting back down again*]:
This is going to provoke a lot of criticism.

[*The song commences. The voice is not particularly strong, but it has great purity and emotion. John Buchanan comes along. He is now a Promethean figure, brilliantly and restlessly alive in a stagnant society. The excess of his power has not yet found a channel. If it remains without one, it will burn him up. At present he is unmarked by the dissipations in which he relieves his demoniac unrest; he*

8

*has the fresh and shining look of an epic hero. He walks
leisurely before the Winemillers' bench, negligently touching the crown of his hat but not glancing at them; climbs
the steps to the base of the fountain, then turns and looks
in the direction of the singer. A look of interest touched
with irony appears on his face. A couple, strolling in the
park, pass behind the fountain.]*

THE GIRL:
Look who's by the fountain!

THE MAN:
Bright as a new silver dollar!

JOHN:
Hi, Dusty! Hi, Pearl!

THE MAN:
How'd you make out in that floating crap game?

JOHN:
I floated with it as far as Vicksburg, then sank.

THE GIRL:
Everybody's been calling: "Johnny, Johnny—where's Johnny?"

*[John's father, Dr. Buchanan, comes on from the right, as
Rev. and Mrs. Winemiller move off the scene to the left,
toward the band music. Dr. Buchanan is an elderly man
whose age shows in his slow and stiff movements. He
walks with a cane. John sees him coming, but pretends
not to and starts to walk off.]*

DR. BUCHANAN:
John!

JOHN *[slowly turning around, as the couple move off]*:
Oh! Hi, Dad. . . . *[They exchange a long look.]* I—uh—
meant to wire you but I must've forgot. I got tied up in

9

Vicksburg Friday night and just now got back to town. Haven't been to the house yet. Is everything . . . going okay? [*He takes a drink of water at the fountain.*]

DR. BUCHANAN [*slowly, in a voice hoarse with emotion*]: There isn't any room in the medical profession for wasters, drunkards and lechers. And there isn't any room in my house for wasters—drunkards—lechers! [*A child is heard calling "I sp-yyyyyy!" in the distance.*] I married late in life. I brought over five hundred children into this world before I had one of my own. And by God it looks like I've given myself the rottenest one of the lot. . . . [*John laughs uncertainly.*] You will find your things at the Alhambra Hotel.

JOHN:
Okay. If that's how you want it.

[*There is a pause. The singing comes through on the music. John tips his hat diffidently and starts away from the fountain. He goes a few feet and his father suddenly calls after him.*]

DR. BUCHANAN:
John! [*John pauses and looks back.*] Come here.

JOHN:
Yes, Sir? [*He walks back to his father and stands before him.*]

DR. BUCHANAN [*hoarsely*]:
Go to the Alhambra Hotel and pick up your things and— bring them back to the house.

JOHN [*gently*]:
Yes, Sir. If that's how you want it. [*He diffidently extends a hand to touch his father's shoulder.*]

DR. BUCHANAN [*brushing the hand roughly off*]:
You! . . . You infernal *whelp*, you!

10

[*Dr. Buchanan turns and goes hurriedly away. John looks after him with a faint, affectionate smile, then sits down on the steps with an air of relief, handkerchief to forehead, and a whistle of relief. Just then the singing at the bandstand ends and there is the sound of applause. Mrs. Winemiller comes in from the left, followed by her husband.*]

MRS. WINEMILLER:
Where is the ice cream man?

MR. WINEMILLER:
Mother, hush! [*He sees his daughter approaching.*] Here we are, Alma!

[*The song ends. There is applause. Then the band strikes up the Santiago Waltz.*

[*Alma Winemiller enters. Alma had an adult quality as a child and now, in her middle twenties, there is something prematurely spinsterish about her. An excessive propriety and self-consciousness is apparent in her nervous laughter; her voice and gestures belong to years of church entertainments, to the position of hostess in a rectory. People her own age regard her as rather quaintly and humorously affected. She has grown up mostly in the company of her elders. Her true nature is still hidden even from herself. She is dressed in pale yellow and carries a yellow silk parasol.*]

[*As Alma passes in front of the fountain, John slaps his hands resoundingly together a few times. She catches her breath in a slight laughing sound, makes as if to retreat, with a startled "Oh!", but then goes quickly to her parents. The applause from the crowd continues.*]

MR. WINEMILLER:
They seem to want to hear you sing again, Alma.

[*She turns nervously about, touching her throat and her chest. John grins, applauding by the fountain. When the applause dies out, Alma sinks faintly on the bench.*]

ALMA:

Open my bag, Father. My fingers have frozen stiff! [*She draws a deep labored breath.*] I don't know what came over me—absolute panic! Never, never again, it isn't worth it— the tortures that I go through!

MR. WINEMILLER [*anxiously*]:

You're having one of your nervous attacks?

ALMA:

My heart's beating so! It seemed to be in my *throat* the whole time I was singing! [*John laughs audibly from the fountain.*] Was it noticeable, Father?

MR. WINEMILLER:

You sang extremely well, Alma. But you know how I feel about this, it was contrary to my wishes and I cannot imagine why you wanted to do it, especially since it seemed to upset you so.

ALMA:

I don't see how anyone could object to my singing at a patriotic occasion. If I had just sung well! But I barely got through it. At one point I thought that I wouldn't. The words flew out of my mind. Did you notice the pause? Blind panic! They really never came back, but I went on singing —I think I must have been improvising the lyric! Whew! Is there a handkerchief in it?

MRS. WINEMILLER [*suddenly*]:

Where is the ice cream man?

ALMA [*rubbing her fingers together*]:

Circulation is slowly coming back . . .

MR. WINEMILLER:
Sit back quietly and take a deep breath, Alma.

ALMA:
Yes, my handkerchief—now . . .

MRS. WINEMILLER:
Where is the ice cream man?

MR. WINEMILLER:
Mother, there isn't any ice cream man.

ALMA:
No, there isn't any ice cream man, Mother. But on the way home Mr. Doremus and I will stop by the drug store and pick up a pint of ice cream.

MR. WINEMILLER:
Are you intending to stay here?

ALMA:
Until the concert is over. I promised Roger I'd wait for him.

MR. WINEMILLER:
I suppose you have noticed who is by the fountain?

ALMA:
Shhh!

MR. WINEMILLER:
Hadn't you better wait on a different bench?

ALMA:
This is where Roger will meet me.

MR. WINEMILLER:
Well, Mother, we'll run along now. [*Mrs. Winemiller has started vaguely toward the fountain, Mr. Winemiller firmly restraining her.*] This way, this way, Mother! [*He takes her arm and leads her off.*]

MRS. WINEMILLER [*calling back, in a high, childish voice*]:

13

Strawberry, Alma. Chocolate, chocolate and strawberry mixed! Not vanilla!

ALMA [*faintly*]:

Yes, yes, Mother—vanilla . . .

MRS. WINEMILLER [*furiously*]:

I said *not* vanilla. [*shouting*] Strawberry!

MR. WINEMILLER [*fiercely*]:

Mother! We're attracting attention. [*He propels her forcibly away.*]

[*John laughs by the fountain. Alma moves her parasol so that it shields her face from him. She leans back closing her eyes. John notices a firecracker by the fountain. He leans over negligently to pick it up. He grins and lights it and tosses it toward Alma's bench. When it goes off she springs up with a shocked cry, letting the parasol drop.*]

JOHN [*jumping up as if outraged*]:

Hey! Hey, you! [*He looks off to the right. Alma sinks back weakly on the bench. John solicitously advances.*] Are you all right?

ALMA:

I can't seem to—catch my breath! Who threw it?

JOHN:

Some little rascal.

ALMA:

Where?

JOHN:

He ran away quick when I hollered!

ALMA:

There ought to be an ordinance passed in this town forbidding firecrackers.

JOHN:

Dad and I treated fifteen kids for burns the last couple of days. I think you need a little restorative, don't you? [*He takes out a flask.*] Here!

ALMA:

What is it?

JOHN:

Apple-jack brandy.

ALMA:

No thank you.

JOHN:

Liquid dynamite.

ALMA:

I'm sure.

[*John laughs and returns it to his pocket. He remains looking down at her with one foot on the end of her bench. His steady, smiling look into her face is disconcerting her.*

[*In Alma's voice and manner there is a delicacy and elegance, a kind of "airiness," which is really natural to her as it is, in a less marked degree, to many Southern girls. Her gestures and mannerisms are a bit exaggerated but in a graceful way. It is understandable that she might be accused of "putting on airs" and of being "affected" by the other young people of the town. She seems to belong to a more elegant age, such as the Eighteenth Century in France. Out of nervousness and self-consciousness she has a habit of prefacing and concluding her remarks with a little breathless laugh. This will be indicated at points, but should be used more freely than indicated; however, the characterization must never be stressed to the point of*

15

making her at all ludicrous in a less than sympathetic way.]

ALMA:

You're—home for the summer? [*John gives an affirmative grunt.*] Summer is not the pleasantest time of year to renew an acquaintance with Glorious Hill—is it? [*John gives an indefinite grunt. Alma laughs airily.*] The Gulf wind has failed us this year, disappointed us dreadfully this summer. We used to be able to rely on the Gulf wind to cool the nights off for us, but this summer has been an exceptional season. [*He continues to grin disconcertingly down at her; she shows her discomfiture in flurried gestures.*]

JOHN [*slowly*]:

Are you—disturbed about something?

ALMA:

That firecracker was a shock.

JOHN:

You should be over that shock by now.

ALMA:

I don't get over shocks quickly.

JOHN:

I see you don't.

ALMA:

You're planning to stay here and take over some of your father's medical practice?

JOHN:

I haven't made up my mind about anything yet.

ALMA:

I hope so, we all hope so. Your father was telling me that you have succeeded in isolating the germ of that fever epidemic that's broken out at Lyon.

JOHN:

Finding something to kill it is more of a trick.

ALMA:

You'll do that! He's so positive that you will. He says that you made a special study of bacter—bacter . . .

JOHN:

Bacteriology!

ALMA:

Yes! At Johns Hopkins! That's in Boston, isn't it?

JOHN:

No. Baltimore.

ALMA:

Oh, Baltimore. Baltimore, Maryland. Such a beautiful combination of names. And bacteriology—isn't that something you do with a microscope?

JOHN:

Well—partly. . . .

ALMA:

I've looked through a telescope, but never a microscope. What . . . what do you—see?

JOHN:

A—universe, Miss Alma.

ALMA:

What kind of a universe?

JOHN:

Pretty much the same kind that you saw through the lens of a telescope—a mysterious one. . . .

ALMA:

Oh, yes. . . .

JOHN:

Part anarchy—and part order!

ALMA:
The footprints of God!

JOHN:
But not God.

ALMA [*ecstatically*]:
To be a doctor! And deal with these mysteries under the microscope lens . . . I think it is more religious than being a priest! There is so much suffering in the world it actually makes one sick to think about it, and most of us are so helpless to relieve it. . . . But a physician! Oh, my! With his magnificent gifts and training what a joy it must be to know that he is equipped and appointed to bring relief to all of this fearful suffering—and fear! And it's an expanding profession, it's a profession that is continually widening its horizons. So many diseases have already come under scientific control but the commencement is just—beginning! I mean there is so much more that is yet to be done, such as mental afflictions to be brought under control. . . . And with your father's example to inspire you! Oh, my!

JOHN:
I didn't know you had so many ideas about the medical profession.

ALMA:
Well, I am a great admirer of your father, as well as a patient. It's such a comfort knowing that he's right next door, within arm's reach as it were!

JOHN:
Why? Do you have fits? . . .

ALMA:
Fits? [*She throws back her head with a peal of gay laughter.*] Why no, but I do have attacks!—of nervous heart

18

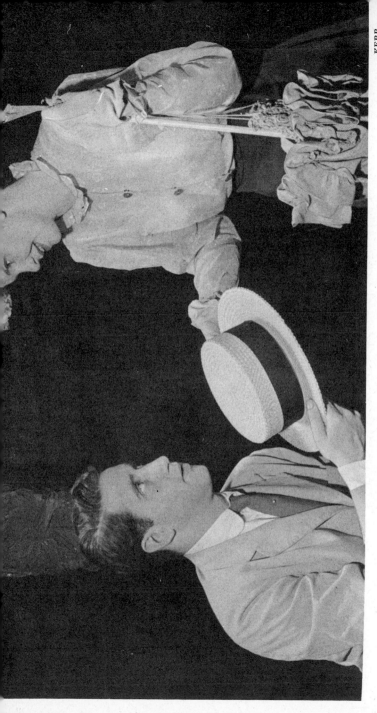

ALMA:
You're planning to stay here and take over some of your
father's medical practice?

JOHN:
I haven't made up my mind about anything yet.

trouble. Which can be so alarming that I run straight to your father!

JOHN:

At two or three in the morning?

ALMA:

Yes, as late as that, even . . . occasionally. He's very patient with me.

JOHN:

But does you no good?

ALMA:

He always reassures me.

JOHN:

Temporarily?

ALMA:

Yes . . .

JOHN:

Don't you want more than that?

ALMA:

What?

JOHN:

It's none of my business.

ALMA:

What were you going to say?

JOHN:

You're Dad's patient. But I have an idea . . .

ALMA:

Please go on! [*John laughs a little.*] Now you have to go on! You can't leave me up in the air! What were you going to tell me?

JOHN:
Only that I suspect you need something more than a little temporary reassurance.

ALMA:
Why? Why? You think it's more serious than . . . ?

JOHN:
You're swallowing air.

ALMA:
I'm what?

JOHN:
You're swallowing air, Miss Alma.

ALMA:
I'm swallowing air?

JOHN:
Yes, you swallow air when you laugh or talk. It's a little trick that hysterical women get into.

ALMA [*uncertainly*]:
Ha-ha . . . !

JOHN:
You swallow air and it presses on your heart and gives you palpitations. That isn't serious in itself but it's a symptom of something that is. Shall I tell you frankly?

ALMA:
Yes!

JOHN:
Well, what I think you have is a *doppelganger!* You have a *doppelganger* and the *doppelganger* is badly irritated.

ALMA:
Oh, my goodness! I have an irritated *doppelganger!* [*She tries to laugh, but is definitely uneasy.*] How awful that sounds! What exactly *is* it?

JOHN:
It's none of *my* business. You are not *my* patient.

ALMA:
But that's downright wicked of you! To tell me I have something awful-sounding as that, and then refuse to let me know what it is! [*She tries to laugh again, unsuccessfully.*]

JOHN:
I shouldn't have said anything! I'm not your doctor. . . .

ALMA:
Just how did you arrive at this—diagnosis of my case? [*She laughs.*] But of course you're teasing me. Aren't you? . . . There, the Gulf wind is stirring! He's actually moving the leaves of the palmetto! And listen to them complaining. . . .

[*As if brought in by this courier from the tropics, Rosa Gonzales enters and crosses to the fountain. Her indolent walk produces a sound and an atmosphere like the Gulf wind on the palmettos, a whispering of silk and a slight rattle of metallic ornaments. She is dressed in an almost outrageous finery, with lustrous feathers on her hat, greenish blue, a cascade of them, also diamond and emerald earrings.*]

JOHN [*sharply*]:
Who is that?

ALMA:
I'm surprised that you don't know.

JOHN:
I've been away quite a while.

ALMA:
That's the Gonzales girl. . . . Her father's the owner of the gambling casino on Moon Lake. [*Rosa drinks at the foun-*

tain and wanders leisurely off.] She smiled at you, didn't she?

JOHN:
I thought she did.

ALMA:
I hope that you have a strong character. [*He places a foot on the end of the bench.*]

JOHN:
Solid rock.

ALMA [*nervously*]:
The pyrotechnical display is going to be brilliant.

JOHN:
The what?

ALMA:
The fireworks.

JOHN:
Aw!

ALMA:
I suppose you've lost touch with most of your *old* friends here.

JOHN [*laconically*]:
Yeah.

ALMA:
You must make some *new* ones! I belong to a little group that meets every ten days. I think you'd enjoy them, too. They're young people with—intellectual and artistic interests. . . .

JOHN [*sadly*]:
Aw, I see . . . intellectual. . . .

ALMA:

You must come!—sometime—I'm going to remind you of
it. . . .

JOHN:

Thanks. Do you mind if I sit down?

ALMA:

Why, certainly not, there's room enough for two! Neither
of us are—terribly large in diameter! [*She laughs shrilly.*]

[*A girl's voice is heard calling: "Goodbye, Nellie!" and
another answers: "Goodbye!" Nellie Ewell enters—a girl
of sixteen with a radiantly fresh healthy quality.*]

ALMA:

Here comes someone much nicer! One of my adorable little
vocal pupils, the youngest and prettiest one with the least
gift for music.

JOHN:

I know that one.

ALMA:

Hello, there, Nellie dear!

NELLIE:

Oh, Miss Alma, your singing was so beautiful it made me
cry.

ALMA:

It's sweet of you to fib so. I sang terribly.

NELLIE:

You're just being modest, Miss Alma. Hello, Dr. John! Dr.
John?

JOHN:

Yeah?

NELLIE:

That book you gave me is too full of long words.

23

JOHN:

Look 'em up in the dictionary, Nellie.

NELLIE:

I did, but you know how dictionaries are. You look up one long word and it gives you another and you look up that one and it gives you the long word you looked up in the first place. [*John laughs.*] I'm coming over tomorrow for you to explain it all to me. [*She laughs and goes off.*]

ALMA:

What book is she talking about?

JOHN:

A book I gave her about the facts of nature. She came over to the office and told me her mother wouldn't tell her anything and she had to know because she'd fallen in love.

ALMA:

Why the precocious little—imp! [*She laughs.*]

JOHN:

What sort of a mother has she?

ALMA:

Mrs. Ewell's the merry widow of Glorious Hill. They say that she goes to the depot to meet every train in order to make the acquaintance of traveling salesmen. Of course she is ostracized by all but a few of her own type of women in town, which is terribly hard for Nellie. It isn't fair to the child. Father didn't want me to take her as a pupil because of her mother's reputation, but I feel that one has a duty to perform toward children in such—circumstances. . . . And I always say that life is such a mysteriously complicated thing that no one should really presume to judge and condemn the behavior of anyone else!

[*There is a faraway "puff" and a burst of golden light over their heads. Both look up. There is a long-drawn*

24

"Ahhh . . ." from the invisible crowd. This is an effect that will be repeated at intervals during the scene.]

There goes the first sky-rocket! Oh, look at it burst into a million stars!

[*John leans way back to look up and allows his knees to spread wide apart so that one of them is in contact with Alma's. The effect upon her is curiously disturbing.*]

JOHN [*after a moment*]:
Do you have a chill?

ALMA:
Why, no!—no. Why?

JOHN:
You're shaking.

ALMA:
Am I?

JOHN:
Don't you feel it?

ALMA:
I have a touch of malaria lingering on.

JOHN:
You have malaria?

ALMA:
Never severely, never really severely. I just have touches of it that come and go. [*She laughs airily.*]

JOHN [*with a gentle grin*]:
Why do you laugh that way?

ALMA:
What way?

[*John imitates her laugh. Alma laughs again in embarrassment.*]

JOHN:
Yeah. That way.

ALMA:
I do declare, you haven't changed in the slightest. It used to delight you to embarrass me and it still does!

JOHN:
I guess I shouldn't tell you this, but I heard an imitation of you at a party.

ALMA:
Imitation? Of what?

JOHN:
You.

ALMA:
I?—I? Why, *what* did they imitate?

JOHN:
You singing at a wedding.

ALMA:
My voice?

JOHN:
Your gestures and facial expression!

ALMA:
How mystifying!

JOHN:
No, I shouldn't have told you. You're upset about it.

ALMA:
I'm not in the least upset, I am just mystified.

JOHN:
Don't you know that you have a reputation for putting on airs a little—for gilding the lily a bit?

ALMA:
I have no idea what you are talking about.

Dr. Buchanan knew his son was a wastrel, knew that Alma
loved him, but his vision was deeper still—he saw the almost
unbridgeable gulf between their moral attitudes.

JOHN:
Well, some people seem to have gotten the idea that you are just a little bit—affected!

ALMA:
Well, well, well, well. [*She tries to conceal her hurt.*] That may be so, it may seem so to some people. But since I am innocent of any attempt at affectation, I really don't know what I can do about it.

JOHN:
You have a rather fancy way of talking.

ALMA:
Have I?

JOHN:
Pyrotechnical display instead of fireworks, and that sort of thing.

ALMA:
So?

JOHN:
And how about that accent?

ALMA:
Accent? This leaves me quite speechless! I have sometimes been accused of having a put-on accent by people who disapprove of good diction. My father was a Rhodes scholar at Oxford, and while over there he fell into the natural habit of using the long A where it is correct to use it. I suppose I must have picked it up from him, but it's entirely unconscious. Who gave this imitation at this party you spoke of?

JOHN [*grinning*]:
I don't think she'd want that told.

ALMA:
Oh, it was a *she* then?

JOHN:

You don't think a man could do it?

ALMA:

No, and I don't think a lady would do it either!

JOHN:

I didn't think it would have made you so mad, or I wouldn't have brought it up.

ALMA:

Oh, I'm not mad. I'm just mystified and amazed as I always am by unprovoked malice in people. I don't understand it when it's directed at me and I don't understand it when it is directed at anybody else. I just don't understand it, and perhaps it is better not to understand it. These people who call me affected and give these unkind imitations of me— I wonder if they stop to think that I have had certain difficulties and disadvantages to cope with—which may be partly the cause of these peculiarities of mine—which they find so offensive!

JOHN:

Now, Miss Alma, you're making a mountain out of a mole-hill!

ALMA:

I wonder if they stop to think that my circumstances are somewhat different from theirs? My father and I have a certain—cross—to bear!

JOHN:

What cross?

ALMA:

Living next door to us, you should know what cross.

JOHN:

Mrs. Winemiller?

ALMA:

She had her breakdown while I was still in high school.
And from that time on I have had to manage the Rectory
and take over the social and household duties that would
ordinarily belong to a minister's wife, not his daughter. And
that may have made me seem strange to some of my more
critical contemporaries. In a way it may have—deprived me
of—my youth. . . .

[*Another rocket goes up. Another "Ahhh . . ." from the
crowd.*]

JOHN:

You ought to go out with young people.

ALMA:

I am not a recluse. I don't fly around here and there giving
imitations of other people at parties. But I am not a recluse
by any manner of means. Being a minister's daughter I have
to be more selective than most girls about the—society I
keep. But I do go out now and then. . . .

JOHN:

I have seen you in the public library and the park, but only
two or three times have I seen you out with a boy and it
was always someone like this Roger Doremus.

ALMA:

I'm afraid that you and I move in different circles. If I
wished to be as outspoken as you are, which is sometimes
just an excuse for being rude—I might say that I've yet to
see you in the company of a—well, a—reputable young
woman. You've heard unfavorable talk about me in your
circle of acquaintances and I've heard equally unpleasant
things about you in mine. And the pity of it is that you
are preparing to be a doctor. You're intending to practice
your father's profession here in Glorious Hill. [*She catches*

29

her breath in a sob.] Most of us have no choice but to lead useless lives! But you have a gift for scientific research! You have a chance to serve humanity. Not just to go on enduring for the sake of endurance, but to serve a noble, humanitarian cause, to relieve human suffering. And what do you do about it? Everything that you can to alienate the confidence of nice people who love and respect your father. While he is devoting himself to the fever at Lyon you drive your automobile at a reckless pace from one disorderly roadhouse to another! You say you have seen two things through the microscope, anarchy and order? Well, obviously *order* is not the thing that impressed you . . . conducting yourself like some overgrown schoolboy who wants to be known as the wildest fellow in town! And you—a gifted young doctor— *Magna cum Laude!* [*She turns aside, touching her eyelids with a handkerchief.*] You know what I call it? I call it a *desecration!* [*She sobs uncontrollably. Then she springs up from the bench. John catches her hand.*]

JOHN:
You're not going to run off, are you?

ALMA:
Singing in public always—always upsets me!—Let go of my hand. [*He holds on to it, grinning up at her in the deepening dusk. The stars are coming out in the cyclorama with its leisurely floating cloud-forms. In the distance the band is playing "La Golondrina."*] Please let go of my hand.

JOHN:
Don't run off mad.

ALMA:
Let's not make a spectacle of ourselves.

JOHN:
Then sit back down.

[*A skyrocket goes up. The crowd "Ahhh . . s."*]

ALMA:

You threw that firecracker and started a conversation just in order to tease me as you did as a child. You came to this bench in order to embarrass me and to hurt my feelings with the report of that vicious—imitation! No, let go of my hand so I can leave, now. You've succeeded in your purpose. I *was* hurt, I *did* make a fool of myself as you intended! So let me go now!

JOHN:

You're attracting attention! Don't you know that I really *like* you, Miss Alma?

ALMA:

No, you don't.

[*Another skyrocket.*]

JOHN:

Sure I do. A lot. Sometimes when I come home late at night I look over at the Rectory. I see something white at the window. Could that be you, Miss Alma? Or, is it your *doppelganger,* looking out of the window that faces my way?

ALMA:

Enough about *doppelganger*—whatever that is!

JOHN:

There goes a nice one, Roman candle they call it!

[*This time the explosion is in back of them. A Roman candle shoots up puffs of rainbow-colored light in back of the stone angel of the fountain. They turn in profile to watch it.*]

JOHN [*counting the puffs of light*]:
Four—five—six—that's all? No—seven! [*There is a pause.
Alma sits down slowly.*]

ALMA [*vaguely*]:
Dear me . . . [*She fans herself.*]

JOHN:
How about going riding?

ALMA [*too eagerly*]:
When . . . now?

[*Rosa Gonzales has wandered up to the fountain again.
John's attention drifts steadily toward her and away from
Alma.*]

JOHN [*too carelessly*]:
Oh . . . some afternoon.

ALMA:
Would you observe the speed limit?

ALMA:
Strictly with you, Miss Alma.

ALMA:
Why then, I'd be glad to—John.

[*John has risen from the bench and crosses to the fountain.*]

JOHN:
And wear a hat with a plume!

ALMA:
I don't have a hat with a plume!

JOHN:
Get one!

[*Another skyrocket goes up, and there is another long
"Ahhh . . ." from the crowd. John saunters up to the*

*fountain. Rosa has lingered beside it. As he passes her
he whispers something. She laughs and moves leisurely
off. John takes a quick drink at the fountain, then follows
Rosa, calling back "Good night" to Alma. There is a
sound of laughter in the distance. Alma sits motionless
for a moment, then touches a small white handkerchief to
her lips and nostrils. Mr. Doremus comes in, carrying a
French horn case. He is a small man, somewhat like a
sparrow.*]

ROGER:
Whew! Golly! Moses! —Well, how did it go, Miss Alma?

ALMA:
How did—what—go?

ROGER [*annoyed*]:
My solo on the French horn.

ALMA [*slowly, without thinking*]:
I paid no attention to it. [*She rises slowly and takes his arm.*]
I'll have to hang on your arm—I'm feeling so dizzy!

[*The scene dims out. There is a final skyrocket and a last
"Ahhh . . ." from the crowd in the distance. Music is
heard, and there is light on the angel.*]

SCENE TWO

Inside the Rectory, which is lighted. Mrs. Winemiller comes in and makes her way stealthily to the love seat, where she seats herself. Opening her parasol, she takes out a fancy white-plumed hat which she had concealed there. Rising, she turns to the mirror on the wall over the love seat and tries on the hat. She draws a long, ecstatic breath as she places it squarely on her head. At that moment the telephone rings. Startled, she snatches off the hat, hides it behind the center table and quickly resumes her seat. The telephone goes on ringing. Alma comes in to answer it.

ALMA:
Hello. . . . Yes, Mr. Gillam. . . . She did? . . . Are you sure? . . . How shocking! . . . [*Mrs. Winemiller now retrieves the hat, seats herself in front of Alma and puts the hat on.*] Thank you, Mr. Gillam . . . the hat is here.

[*Mr. Winemiller comes in. He is distracted.*]

MR. WINEMILLER:
Alma! Alma, your mother . . . !

ALMA [*coming in*]:
I know, Father, Mr. Gillam just phoned. He told me she picked up a white plumed hat and he pretended not to notice in order to save you the embarrassment, so I—I told him to just charge it to us.

MR. WINEMILLER:
That hat looks much too expensive.

ALMA:
It's fourteen dollars. You pay six of it, Father, and I'll pay eight. [*She gives him the parasol.*]

MR. WINEMILLER:

What an insufferable cross we have to bear. [*He retires despairingly from the room.*]

[*Alma goes over to her mother and seats her in a chair at the table.*]

ALMA:

I have a thousand and one things to do before my club meeting tonight, so you work quietly on your picture puzzle or I shall take the hat back, plume and all.

MRS. WINEMILLER [*throwing a piece of the puzzle on the floor*]:

The pieces don't fit! [*Alma picks up the piece and puts it on the table.*] The pieces don't fit!

[*Alma stands for a moment in indecision. She reaches for the phone, then puts it down. Then she takes it up again, and gives a number. The telephone across the way in the doctor's office rings and that part of the scene lights up. John comes in.*]

JOHN [*answering the phone*]:

Hello?

ALMA:

John! [*She fans herself rapidly with a palm leaf clutched in her free hand and puts on a brilliant, strained smile as if she were actually in his presence.*]

JOHN:

Miss Alma?

ALMA:

You recognized my voice?

JOHN:

I recognized your laugh.

ALMA:

Ha-ha! How are you, you stranger you?

JOHN:

I'm pretty well, Miss Alma. How're you doing?

ALMA:

Surviving, just surviving! Isn't it fearful?

JOHN:

Uh-huh.

ALMA:

You seem unusually laconic. Or perhaps I should say more than usually laconic.

JOHN:

I had a big night and I'm just recovering from it.

ALMA:

Well, sir, I have a bone to pick with you!

JOHN:

What's that, Miss Alma? [*He drains a glass of bromo.*]

ALMA:

The time of our last conversation on the Fourth of July, you said you were going to take me riding in your automobile.

JOHN:

Aw. Did I say that?

ALMA:

Yes indeed you did, sir! And all these hot afternoons I've been breathlessly waiting and hoping that you would remember that promise. But now I know how insincere you are. Ha-ha! Time and again the four-wheeled phenomenon flashes by the Rectory and I have yet to put my—my quaking foot in it!

[*Mrs. Winemiller begins to mock Alma's speech and laughter.*]

JOHN:

What was that, Miss Alma? I didn't understand you.

ALMA:

I was just reprimanding you, sir! Castigating you verbally! Ha-ha!

MRS. WINEMILLER [*grimacing*]:
Ha-ha.

JOHN:

What about, Miss Alma? [*He leans back and puts his feet on table.*]

ALMA:

Never mind. I know how busy you are! [*She whispers.*] Mother, *hush!*

JOHN:

I'm afraid we have a bad connection.

ALMA:

I hate telephones. I don't know why but they always make me laugh as if someone were poking me in the ribs! I swear to goodness they do!

JOHN:

Why don't you just go to your window and I'll go to mine and we can holler across?

ALMA:

The yard's so wide I'm afraid it would crack my voice! And I've got to sing at somebody's wedding tomorrow.

JOHN:

You're going to sing at a wedding?

ALMA:

Yes. "The Voice That Breathed O'er Eden!" And I'm

as hoarse as a frog! [*Another gale of laughter almost shakes her off her feet.*]

JOHN:
Better come over and let me give you a gargle.

ALMA:
Nasty gargles—I hate them!

MRS. WINEMILLER [*mockingly*]:
Nasty gargles—I hate them!

ALMA:
Mother, shhh!—please! As you no doubt have gathered, there is some interference at this end of the line! What I wanted to say is—you remember my mentioning that little club I belong to?

JOHN:
Aw! Aw, yes! Those intellectual meetings!

ALMA:
Oh, now, don't call it that. It's just a little informal gathering every Wednesday and we talk about the new books and read things out loud to each other!

JOHN:
Serve any refreshments?

ALMA:
Yes, we serve refreshments!

JOHN:
Any liquid refreshments?

ALMA:
Both liquid and solid refreshments.

JOHN:
Is this an invitation?

ALMA:
Didn't I promise I'd ask you? It's going to be tonight!—at

ALMA:
Hush, Mother—be quiet . . . at least until I get John to promise to come over without fail!

eight at my house, at the Rectory, so all you'll have to do is cross the yard!

JOHN:

I'll try to make it, Miss Alma.

ALMA:

Don't say try as if it required some Herculean effort! All you have to do is . . .

JOHN:

Cross the yard! Uh-huh—reserve me a seat by the punch bowl.

ALMA:

That gives me an idea! We *will* have punch, fruit punch, with claret in it. Do you like claret?

JOHN:

I just dote on claret.

ALMA:

Now you're being sarcastic! Ha-ha-ha!

JOHN:

Excuse me, Miss Alma, but Dad's got to use this phone.

ALMA:

I won't hang up till you've said you'll come without fail!

JOHN:

I'll be there, Miss Alma. You can count on it.

ALMA:

Au revoir, then! Until eight.

JOHN:

G'bye, Miss Alma.

[*John hangs up with an incredulous grin. Alma remains holding the phone with a dazed smile until the office interior has dimmed slowly out.*]

39

MRS. WINEMILLER:

Alma's in love—in love. [*She waltzes mockingly.*]

ALMA [*sharply*]:

Mother, you are wearing out my patience! Now I am expecting another music pupil and I have to make preparations for the club meeting so I suggest that you . . . [*Nellie rings the bell.*] Will you go up to your room? [*Then she calls sweetly.*] Yes, Nellie, coming, Nellie. All right, stay down here then. But keep your attention on your picture puzzle or there will be no ice cream for you after supper!

[*She admits Nellie, who is wildly excited over something. This scene should be played lightly and quickly.*]

NELLIE:

Oh, Miss Alma!

[*She rushes past Alma in a distracted manner, throws herself on the sofa and hugs herself with excited glee.*]

ALMA:

What is it, Nellie? Has something happened at home? [*Nellie continues her exhilaration.*] Oh, now, Nellie, stop that! Whatever it is, it can't be *that* important!

NELLIE [*blurting out suddenly*]:

Miss Alma, haven't you ever had—*crushes*?

ALMA:

What?

NELLIE:

Crushes?

ALMA:

Yes—I suppose I have. [*She sits down.*]

NELLIE:

Did you know that I used to have a crush on *you*, Miss Alma?

ALMA:

No, Nellie.

NELLIE:

Why do you think that I took singing lessons?

ALMA:

I supposed it was because you wished to develop your voice.

NELLIE [*cutting in*]:

Oh, you know, and I know, I never had any voice. I had a crush on you though. Those were the days when I had crushes on girls. Those days are all over, and now I have crushes on boys. Oh, Miss Alma, you know about Mother, how I was brought up so nobody nice except you would have anything to do with us—Mother meeting the trains to pick up the traveling salesmen and bringing them home to drink and play poker—all of them acting like pigs, pigs, pigs!

MRS. WINEMILLER [*mimicking*]:

Pigs, pigs, pigs!

NELLIE:

Well, I thought I'd always hate men. Loathe and despise them. But last night— Oh!

ALMA:

Hadn't we better run over some scales until you are feeling calmer?

NELLIE [*cutting in*]:

I'd heard them downstairs for hours but didn't know who it was—I'd fallen asleep—when all of a sudden my door banged open. He'd thought it was the bathroom!

ALMA [*nervously*]:

Nellie, I'm not sure I want to hear any more of this story.

NELLIE [*interrupting*]:
Guess who it was?

ALMA:
I couldn't possibly guess.

NELLIE:
Someone you know. Someone I've seen you with.

ALMA:
Who?

NELLIE:
The wonderfullest person in all the big wide world! When
he saw it was me he came and sat down on the bed and
held my hand and we talked and talked until Mother came
up to see what had happened to him. You should have heard
him bawl her out. Oh, he laid the law down! He said she
ought to send me off to a girl's school because she wasn't fit
to bring up a daughter! Then she started to bawl him out.
You're a fine one to talk, she said, you're not fit to call
yourself a doctor. [*Alma rises abruptly.*]

ALMA:
John Buchanan?

NELLIE:
Yes, of course, Dr. Johnny.

ALMA:
Was—with—your—mother?

NELLIE:
Oh, he wasn't her beau! He had a girl with him, and
Mother had somebody else!

ALMA:
Who—did—he—have?

NELLIE:
Oh, some loud tacky thing with a Z in her name!

ALMA:

Gonzales? Rosa Gonzales?

NELLIE:

Yes, that was it! [*Alma sits slowly back down.*] But him! Oh, Miss Alma! He's the *wonderfullest* person that I . . .

ALMA [*interrupting*]:

Your mother was right! He isn't fit to call himself a doctor! I hate to disillusion you, but this wonderfullest person is pitiably weak.

[*Someone calls "Johnny" outside.*]

NELLIE [*in hushed excitement*]:

Someone is calling him now!

ALMA:

Yes, these people who shout his name in front of his house are of such a character that the old doctor cannot permit them to come inside the door. And when they have brought him home at night, left him sprawling on the front steps, sometimes at daybreak—it takes two people, his father and the old cook, one pushing and one pulling, to get him upstairs. [*She sits down.*] All the gifts of the gods were showered on him. . . . [*The call of "Johnny" is repeated.*] But all he cares about is indulging his senses! [*Another call of "Johnny."*]

NELLIE:

Here he comes down the steps! [*Alma crosses toward the window.*] Look at him jump!

ALMA:

Oh.

NELLIE:

Over the banisters. Ha-ha!

43

ALMA:

Nellie, don't lean out the window and have us caught spying.

MRS. WINEMILLER [*suddenly*]:

Show Nellie how *you* spy on him! Oh, she's a good one at spying. She stands behind the curtain and *peeks* around it, and . . .

ALMA [*frantically*]:
Mother!

MRS. WINEMILLER:

She spies on him. Whenever he comes in at night she rushes downstairs to watch him out of this window!

ALMA [*interrupting her*]:
Be still!

MRS. WINEMILLER [*going right on*]:

She called him just now and had a fit on the telephone! [*The old lady cackles derisively. Alma snatches her cigarette from her and crushes it under her foot.*] Alma's in love! Alma's in love!

ALMA [*interrupting*]:
Nellie, Nellie, please go.

NELLIE [*with a startled giggle*]:

All right, Miss Alma, I'm going. [*She crosses quickly to the door, looking back once with a grin.*] Good night, Mrs. Winemiller!

[*Nellie goes out gaily, leaving the door slightly open. Alma rushes to it and slams it shut. She returns swiftly to Mrs. Winemiller, her hands clenched with anger.*]

ALMA:

If ever I hear you say such a thing again, if ever you dare to repeat such a thing in my presence or anybody else's—

44

then it will be the last straw! You understand me? Yes, you understand me! You act like a child, but you have the devil in you. And God will punish you—yes! I'll punish you too. I'll take your cigarettes from you and give you no more. I'll give you no ice cream either. Because I'm tired of your malice. Yes, I'm tired of your malice and your self-indulgence. People wonder why I'm tied down here! They pity me—think of me as an old maid already! In spite of I'm young. Still young! It's you—it's you, you've taken my youth away from me! I wouldn't say that—I'd try not even to think it—if you were just kind, just simple! But I could spread my life out like a rug for you to step on and you'd step on it, and not even say "Thank you, Alma!" Which is what you've done always—and now you dare to tell a disgusting lie about me—in front of that girl!

MRS. WINEMILLER:
Don't you think I hear you go to the window at night to watch him come in and . . .

ALMA:
Give me that plumed hat, Mother! It goes back now, it goes back!

MRS. WINEMILLER:
Fight! Fight!

[*Alma snatches at the plumed hat. Mrs. Winemiller snatches too. The hat is torn between them. Mrs. Winemiller retains the hat. The plume comes loose in Alma's hand. She stares at it a moment with a shocked expression.*]

ALMA [*sincerely*]:
Heaven have mercy upon us!

SCENE THREE

Inside the Rectory.

The meeting is in progress, having just opened with the reading of the minutes by Alma. She stands before the green plush sofa and the others. This group includes Mr. Doremus, Vernon, a willowy younger man with an open collar and Byronic locks, the widow Bassett, and a wistful older girl with a long neck and thick-lensed glasses.

ALMA [*reading*]:
Our last meeting which fell on July fourteenth . . .

MRS. BASSETT:
Bastille Day!

ALMA:
Pardon me?

MRS. BASSETT:
It fell on Bastille Day! But, honey, that was the meeting before last.

ALMA:
You're perfectly right. I seem to be on the wrong page. . . . [*She drops the papers.*]

MRS. BASSETT:
Butterfingers!

ALMA:
Here we are! July twenty-fifth! Correct?

MRS. BASSETT:
Correct! [*A little ripple of laughter goes about the circle.*]

ALMA [*continuing*]:
It was debated whether or not we ought to suspend opera-

tions for the remainder of the summer as the departure of several members engaged in the teaching profession for their summer vacations . . .

MRS. BASSETT:
Lucky people!

ALMA:
. . . had substantially contracted our little circle.

MRS. BASSETT:
Decimated our ranks! [*There is another ripple of laughter.*]

[*John appears outside the door-frame and rings the bell.*]

ALMA [*with agitation*]:
Is that—is that—the doorbell?

MRS. BASSETT:
It sure did sound like it to me.

ALMA:
Excuse me a moment. I think it may be . . .

[*She crosses to the door-frame and makes the gesture of opening the door. John steps in, immaculately groomed and shining, his white linen coat over his arm and a white Panama hat in his hand. He is a startling contrast to the other male company, who seem to be outcasts of a state in which he is a prominent citizen.*]

ALMA [*shrilly*]:
Yes, it is—our guest of honor! Everybody, this is Dr. John Buchanan, Jr.

JOHN [*easily glancing about the assemblage*]:
Hello, everybody.

MRS. BASSETT:
I never thought he'd show up. Congratulations, Miss Alma.

47

JOHN:

Did I miss much?

ALMA:

Not a thing! Just the minutes—I'll put you on the sofa. Next to me. [*She laughs breathlessly and makes an uncertain gesture. He settles gingerly on the sofa. They all stare at him with a curious sort of greediness.*] Well, now! we are completely assembled!

MRS. BASSETT [*eagerly*]:

Vernon has his verse play with him tonight!

ALMA [*uneasily*]:

Is that right, Vernon? [*Obviously, it is. Vernon has a pile of papers eight inches thick on his knees. He raises them timidly with downcast eyes.*]

ROGER [*quickly*]:

We decided to put that off till cooler weather. Miss Rosemary is supposed to read us a paper tonight on William Blake.

MRS. BASSETT:

Those dead poets can keep!

[*John laughs.*]

ALMA [*excitedly jumping up*]:

Mrs. Bassett, everybody! This is the way I feel about the verse play. It's too important a thing to read under any but ideal circumstances. Not only atmospheric—on some cool evening with music planned to go with it!—but everyone present so that nobody will miss it! Why don't we . . .

ROGER:

Why don't we take a standing vote on the matter?

ALMA:

Good, good, perfect!

48

ROGER:

All in favor of putting the verse play off till cooler weather, stand up!

[*Everybody rises but Rosemary and Mrs. Bassett. Rosemary starts vaguely to rise, but Mrs. Bassett jerks her arm.*]

ROSEMARY:

Was this a vote?

ROGER:

Now, Mrs. Bassett, no rough tactics, please!

ALMA:

Has everybody got fans? John, you haven't got one!

[*She looks about for a fan for him. Not seeing one, she takes Roger's out of his hand and gives it to John. Roger is non-plussed. Rosemary gets up with her paper.*]

ROSEMARY:

The poet—William Blake.

MRS. BASSETT:

Insane, insane, that man was a mad fanatic! [*She squints her eyes tight shut and thrusts her thumbs into her ears. The reactions range from indignant to conciliatory.*]

ROGER:

Now, Mrs. Bassett!

MRS. BASSETT:

This is a free country. I can speak my opinion. And I have *read up* on him. Go on, Rosemary. I wasn't criticizing your paper. [*But Rosemary sits down, hurt.*]

ALMA:

Mrs. Bassett is only joking, Rosemary.

ROSEMARY:

No, I don't want to read it if she feels that strongly about it.

49

MRS. BASSETT:

Not a bit, don't be silly! I just don't see why we should encourage the writings of people like that who have already gone into a drunkard's grave!

VARIOUS VOICES [*exclaiming*]:

Did he? I never heard that about him. Is that true?

ALMA:

Mrs. Bassett is mistaken about that. Mrs. Bassett, you have confused Blake with someone else.

MRS. BASSETT [*positively*]:

Oh, no, don't tell me. I've read up on him and know what I'm talking about. He traveled around with that Frenchman who took a shot at him and landed them both in jail! Brussels, Brussels!

ROGER [*gaily*]:

Brussels sprouts!

MRS. BASSETT:

That's where it happened, fired a gun at him in a drunken stupor, and later one of them died of T.B. in the gutter! All right. I'm finished. I won't say anything more. Go on with your paper, Rosemary. There's nothing like contact with culture!

[*Alma gets up.*]

ALMA:

Before Rosemary reads her paper on Blake, I think it would be a good idea, since some of us aren't acquainted with his work, to preface the critical and biographical comments with a reading of one of his loveliest lyric poems.

ROSEMARY:

I'm not going to read anything at all! Not I!

John keeps his promise to Alma and attends an intellectual
gathering at her home—uneasy, and fighting boredom,
John knows he'll never last through the reading on the poet
William Blake...

ALMA:

Then let me read it then. [*She takes a paper from Rosemary.*] . . . This is called "Love's Secret."

[*She clears her throat and waits for a hush to settle. Rosemary looks stonily at the carpet. Mrs. Bassett looks at the ceiling. John coughs.*]

> Never seek to tell thy love,
> Love that never told can be,
> For the gentle wind doth move
> Silently, invisibly.
> I told my love, I told my love,
> I told him all my heart.
> Trembling, cold in ghastly fear
> Did my love depart.
>
> No sooner had he gone from me
> Than a stranger passing by,
> Silently, invisibly,
> Took him with a sigh!

[*There are various effusions and enthusiastic applause.*]

MRS. BASSETT:

Honey, you're right. That isn't the man I meant. I was thinking about the one who wrote about "the bought red lips." Who was it that wrote about the "bought red lips"?

[*John has risen abruptly. He signals to Alma and points to his watch. He starts to leave.*]

ALMA [*springing up*]:
John!

JOHN [*calling back*]:
I have to call on a patient!

ALMA:

Oh, John!

[*She calls after him so sharply that the group is startled into silence.*]

ROSEMARY [*interpreting this as a cue to read her paper*]: "The poet, William Blake, was born in 1757 . . ."

[*Alma suddenly rushes to the door and goes out after John.*]

ROGER:

Of poor but honest parents.

MRS. BASSETT:

No supercilious comments out of you, sir. Go on Rosemary. [*She speaks loudly.*] She has such a beautiful *voice!*

[*Alma returns inside, looking stunned.*]

ALMA:

Please excuse the interruption, Rosemary. Dr. Buchanan had to call on a patient.

MRS. BASSETT [*archly*]:

I bet I know who the patient was. Ha-ha! That Gonzales girl whose father owns Moon Lake Casino and goes everywhere with two pistols strapped on his belt. Johnny Buchanan will get himself shot in that crowd!

ALMA:

Why, Mrs. Bassett, what gave you such an idea? I don't think that John even knows that Gonzales girl!

MRS. BASSETT:

He knows her, all right. In the Biblical sense of the word, if you'll excuse me!

ALMA:

No, I will not excuse you! A thing like that is inexcusable!

MRS. BASSETT:

Have you fallen for him, Miss Alma? Miss Alma has fallen for the young doctor! They tell me he has lots of new lady patients!

ALMA:

Stop it! [*She stamps her foot furiously and crushes the palm leaf fan between her clenched hands.*] I won't have malicious talk here! You drove him away from the meeting after I'd bragged so much about how bright and interesting you all were! You put your worst foot forward and simpered and chattered and carried on like idiots, idiots! What am I saying? I—I—please excuse me!

[*She rushes out the inner door.*]

ROGER:

I move that the meeting adjourn.

MRS. BASSETT:

I second the motion.

ROSEMARY:

I don't understand. What happened?

MRS. BASSETT:

Poor Miss Alma!

ROGER:

She hasn't been herself lately. . . .

[*They all go out. After a moment Alma reenters with a tray of refreshments, looks about the deserted interior and bursts into hysterical laughter. The light dims out.*]

SCENE FOUR

In the doctor's office.

John has a wound on his arm which he is bandaging with Rosa's assistance.

JOHN:
Hold that end. Wrap it around. Pull it tight.

[*There is a knock at the door. They look up silently. The knock is repeated.*]

I better answer before they wake up the old man.

[*He goes out. A few moments later he returns followed by Alma. He is rolling down his sleeve to conceal the bandage. Alma stops short at the sight of Rosa.*]

Wait outside, Rosa. In the hall. But be quiet!

[*Rosa gives Alma a challenging look as she withdraws from the lighted area. John explains about Rosa.*]

A little emergency case.

ALMA:
The patient you had to call on. [*John grins.*] I want to see your father.

JOHN:
He's asleep. Anything I can do?

ALMA:
No, I think not. I have to see your father.

JOHN:
It's 2 A.M., Miss Alma.

ALMA:

I know, I'm afraid I'll have to see him.

JOHN:

What's the trouble?

[*The voice of John's father is heard, calling from above.*]

DR. BUCHANAN:

John! What's going on down there?

JOHN [*at the door*]:

Nothing much, Dad. Somebody got cut in a fight.

DR. BUCHANAN:

I'm coming down.

JOHN:

No. Don't! Stay in bed! [*He rolls up his sleeve to show Alma the bandaged wound. She gasps and touches her lips.*] I've patched him up, Dad. You sleep!

[JOHN *executes the gesture of closing a door quietly on the hall.*]

ALMA:

You've been in a brawl with that—woman! [*John nods and rolls the sleeve back down. Alma sinks faintly into a chair.*]

JOHN:

Is your *doppelganger* cutting up again?   •

ALMA:

It's your father I want to talk to.

JOHN:

Be reasonable, Miss Alma. You're not that sick.

ALMA:

Do you suppose I would come here at two o'clock in the morning if I were not seriously ill?

JOHN:

It's no telling what you would do in a state of hysteria. [*He puts some powders in a glass of water.*] Toss that down, Miss Alma.

ALMA:

What is it?

JOHN:

A couple of little white tablets dissolved in water.

ALMA:

What kind of tablets?

JOHN:

You don't trust me?

ALMA:

You are not in any condition to inspire much confidence. [*John laughs softly. She looks at him helplessly for a moment, then bursts into tears. He draws up a chair beside hers and puts his arm gently about her shoulders.*] I seem to be all to pieces.

JOHN:

The intellectual meeting wore you out.

ALMA:

You made a quick escape from it.

JOHN:

I don't like meetings. The only meetings I like are between two people.

ALMA:

Such as between yourself and the lady outside?

JOHN:

Or between you and me.

ALMA [*nervously*]:

Where is the . . . ?

JOHN:

Oh. You've decided to take it?

ALMA:

Yes, if you . . .

[*She sips and chokes. He gives her his handkerchief. She touches her lips with it.*]

JOHN:

Bitter?

ALMA:

Awfully bitter.

JOHN:

It'll make you sleepy.

ALMA:

I do hope so. I wasn't able to sleep.

JOHN:

And you felt panicky?

ALMA:

Yes. I felt walled in.

JOHN:

You started hearing your heart?

ALMA:

Yes, like a drum!

JOHN:

It scared you?

ALMA:

It always does.

JOHN:

Sure. I know.

ALMA:

I don't think I will be able to get through the summer.

JOHN:

You'll get through it, Miss Alma.

ALMA:

How?

JOHN:

One day will come after another and one night will come after another till sooner or later the summer will be all through with and then it will be fall, and you will be saying, I don't see how I'm going to get through the fall.

ALMA:

Oh . . .

JOHN:

That's right. Draw a deep breath!

ALMA:

Ah . . .

JOHN:

Good. Now draw another!

ALMA:

Ah . . .

JOHN:

Better? Better?

ALMA:

A little.

JOHN:

Soon you'll be much better. [*He takes out a big silver watch and holds her wrist.*] Did y' know that time is one side of the four-dimensional continuum we're caught in?

ALMA:

What?

JOHN:

Did you know space is curved, that it turns back onto itself

like a soap-bubble, adrift in something that's even less than
space. [*He laughs a little as he replaces the watch.*]

ROSA [*faintly from outside*]:
Johnny!

JOHN [*looking up as if the cry came from there*]:
Did you know that the Magellanic clouds are a hundred
thousand light years away from the earth? No? [*Alma
shakes her head slightly.*] That's something to think about
when you worry over your heart, that little red fist that's
got to keep knocking, knocking against the big black door.

ROSA [*more distinctly*]:
Johnny!

[*She opens the door a crack.*]

JOHN:
Calla de la boca! [*The door closes and he speaks to Alma.*]
There's nothing wrong with your heart but a little functional disturbance, like I told you before. You want me to
check it? [*Alma nods mutely. John picks up his stethoscope.*]

ALMA:
The lady outside, I hate to keep her waiting.

JOHN:
Rosa doesn't mind waiting. Unbutton your blouse.

ALMA:
Unbutton . . .?

JOHN:
The blouse.

ALMA:
Hadn't I better—better come back in the morning, when
your father will be able to . . . ?

JOHN:

Just as you please, Miss Alma. [*She hesitates. Then begins to unbutton her blouse. Her fingers fumble.*] Fingers won't work?

ALMA [*breathlessly*]:

They are just as if frozen!

JOHN [*smiling*]:

Let me. [*He leans over her.*] Little pearl buttons . . .

ALMA:

If your father discovered that woman in the house . . .

JOHN:

He won't discover it.

ALMA:

It would distress him terribly.

JOHN:

Are you going to tell him?

ALMA:

Certainly not! [*He laughs and applies the stethoscope to her chest.*]

JOHN:

Breathe! . . . Out! . . . Breathe! . . . Out!

ALMA:

Ah . . .

JOHN:

Um-hmmm . . .

ALMA:

What do you hear?

JOHN:

Just a little voice saying—"Miss Alma is lonesome!" [*She rises and turns her back to him.*]

ALMA:

If your idea of helping a patient is to ridicule and insult . . .

JOHN:

My idea of helping you is to tell you the truth. [*Alma looks up at him. He lifts her hand from the chair arm.*] What is this stone?

ALMA:

A topaz.

JOHN:

Beautiful stone. . . . Fingers still frozen?

ALMA:

A little. [*He lifts her hand to his mouth and blows his breath on her fingers.*]

JOHN:

I'm a poor excuse for a doctor, I'm much too selfish. But let's try to think about you.

ALMA:

Why should you bother about me? [*She sits down.*]

JOHN:

You know I like you and I think you're worth a lot of consideration.

ALMA:

Why?

JOHN:

Because you have a lot of feeling in your heart, and that's a rare thing. It makes you too easily hurt. Did I hurt you tonight?

ALMA:

You hurt me when you sprang up from the sofa and rushed from the Rectory in such—in such mad haste that you left your coat behind you!

JOHN:

I'll pick up the coat sometime.

ALMA:

The time of our last conversation you said you would take me riding in your automobile sometime, but you forgot to.

JOHN:

I didn't forget. Many's the time I've looked across at the Rectory and wondered if it would be worth trying, you and me. . . .

ALMA:

You decided it wasn't?

JOHN:

I went there tonight, but it wasn't you and me. . . . Fingers warm now?

ALMA:

Those tablets work quickly. I'm already feeling drowsy. [*She leans back with her eyes nearly shut.*] I'm beginning to feel almost like a water lily. A water lily on a Chinese lagoon.

[*A heavy iron bell strikes three.*]

ROSA:

Johnny?

[*Alma starts to rise.*]

ALMA:

I *must* go.

JOHN:

I will call for you Saturday night at eight o'clock.

ALMA:

What?

JOHN:

I'll give you this box of tablets but watch how you take them. Never more than one or two at a time.

ALMA:

Didn't you say something else a moment ago?

JOHN:

I said I would call for you at the Rectory Saturday night.

ALMA:

Oh . . .

JOHN:

Is that all right? [*Alma nods speechlessly. She remains with the box resting in the palm of her hand as if not knowing it was there. John gently closes her fingers on the box.*]

ALMA:

Oh! [*She laughs faintly.*]

ROSA [*outside*]:
Johnny!

JOHN:

Do you think you can find your way home, Miss Alma?

[*Rosa steps back into the office with a challenging look. Alma catches her breath sharply and goes out the side door.*]

[*John reaches above him and turns out the light. He crosses to Rosa by the anatomy chart and takes her roughly in his arms. The light lingers on the chart as the interior dims out.*]

SCENE FIVE

In the Rectory.

Before the light comes up a soprano voice is heard singing "From the Land of the Sky Blue Waters."

As the curtain rises, Alma gets up from the piano. Mr. and Mrs. Winemiller, also, are in the lighted room.

ALMA:
What time is it, Father? [*He goes on writing. She raises her voice.*] What time is it, Father?

MR. WINEMILLER:
Five of eight. I'm working on my sermon.

ALMA:
Why don't you work in the study?

MR. WINEMILLER:
The study is suffocating. So don't disturb me.

ALMA:
Would there be any chance of getting Mother upstairs if someone should call?

MR. WINEMILLER:
Are you expecting a caller?

ALMA:
Not expecting. There is just a chance of it.

MR. WINEMILLER:
Whom are you expecting?

ALMA:
I said I wasn't expecting anyone, that there was just a possibility . . .

MR. WINEMILLER:

Mr. Doremus? I thought that this was his evening with his mother?

ALMA:

Yes, it is his evening with his mother.

MR. WINEMILLER:

Then who is coming here, Alma?

ALMA:

Probably no one. Probably no one at all.

MR. WINEMILLER:

This is all very mysterious.

MRS. WINEMILLER:

That tall boy next door is coming to see her, that's who's coming to see her.

ALMA:

If you will go upstairs, Mother, I'll call the drug store and ask them to deliver a pint of fresh peach ice cream.

MRS. WINEMILLER:

I'll go upstairs when I'm ready—good and ready, and you can put that in your pipe and smoke it, Miss Winemiller!

[*She lights a cigarette. Mr. Winemiller turns slowly away with a profound sigh.*]

ALMA:

I may as well tell you who might call, so that if he calls there will not be any unpleasantness about it. Young Dr. John Buchanan said he might call.

MRS. WINEMILLER:

See!

MR. WINEMILLER:

You can't be serious.

MRS. WINEMILLER:
Didn't I tell you?

ALMA:
Well, I am.

MR. WINEMILLER:
That young man might come here?

ALMA:
He asked me if he might and I said, yes, if he wished to. But it is now after eight so it doesn't look like he's coming.

MR. WINEMILLER:
If he does come you will go upstairs to your room and I will receive him.

ALMA:
If he does come I'll do no such thing, Father.

MR. WINEMILLER:
You must be out of your mind.

ALMA:
I'll receive him myself. You may retire to your study and Mother upstairs. But if he comes I'll receive him. I don't judge people by the tongues of gossips. I happen to know that he has been grossly misjudged and misrepresented by old busybodies who're envious of his youth and brilliance and charm!

MR. WINEMILLER:
If you're not out of your senses, then I'm out of mine.

ALMA:
I daresay we're all a bit peculiar, Father. . . .

MR. WINEMILLER:
Well, I have had one almost insufferable cross to bear and perhaps I can bear another. But if you think I'm retiring into my study when this young man comes, probably with

a whiskey bottle in one hand and a pair of dice in the other, you have another think coming. I'll sit right here and look at him until he leaves. [*He turns back to his sermon.*]

[*A whistle is heard outside the open door.*]

ALMA [*speaking quickly*]:
As a matter of fact I think I'll walk down to the drug store and call for the ice cream myself. [*She crosses to the door, snatching up her hat, gloves and veil.*]

MRS. WINEMILLER:
There she goes to him! Ha-ha! [*Alma rushes out.*]

MR. WINEMILLER [*looking up*]:
Alma! Alma!

MRS. WINEMILLER:
Ha-ha-haaaaa!

MR. WINEMILLER:
Where is Alma?—Alma! [*He rushes through the door.*]
Alma!

MRS. WINEMILLER:
Ha-ha! Who got fooled? Who got fooled! Ha-haaaa! Insufferable cross yourself, you old—windbag. . . .

[*The curtain comes down.*]

A delicately suggested arbor, enclosing a table and two chairs. Over the table is suspended a torn paper lantern. This tiny set may be placed way downstage in front of the two interiors, which should be darkened out, as in the fountain scenes. In the background, as it is throughout the play, the angel of the fountain is dimly visible.

Music from the nearby pavilion of the Casino can be used when suitable for background.

John's voice is audible before he and Alma enter.

JOHN [*from the darkness*]:
I don't understand why we can't go in the casino.

ALMA:
You do understand. You're just pretending not to.

JOHN:
Give me one reason.

ALMA [*coming into the arbor*]:
I am a minister's daughter.

JOHN:
That's no reason. [*He follows her in. He wears a white linen suit, carrying the coat over his arm.*]

ALMA:
You're a doctor. That's a better reason. You can't any more afford to be seen in such places than I can—less!

JOHN [*bellowing*]:
Dusty!

DUSTY [*from the darkness*]:
Coming!

JOHN:

What are you fishing in that pocketbook for?

ALMA:

Nothing.

JOHN:

What have you got there?

ALMA:

Let go!

JOHN:

Those sleeping tablets I gave you?

ALMA:

Yes.

JOHN:

What for?

ALMA:

I need one.

JOHN:

Now?

ALMA:

Yes.

JOHN:

Why?

ALMA:

Why? Because I nearly died of heart failure in your automobile. What possessed you to drive like that? A demon?

[*Dusty enters.*]

JOHN:

A bottle of vino rosso.

DUSTY:

Sure. [*He withdraws.*]

69

JOHN:

Hey! Tell Shorty I want to hear the "Yellow Dog Blues."

ALMA:

Please give me back my tablets.

JOHN:

You want to turn into a dope-fiend taking this stuff? I said take one when you need one.

ALMA:

I need one now.

JOHN:

Sit down and stop swallowing air. [*Dusty returns with a tall wine bottle and two thin-stemmed glasses.*] When does the cock-fight start?

DUSTY:

'Bout ten o'clock, Dr. Johnny.

ALMA:

When does *what start?*

JOHN:

They have a cock-fight here every Saturday night. Ever seen one?

ALMA:

Perhaps in some earlier incarnation of mine.

JOHN:

When you wore a brass ring in your nose?

ALMA:

Then maybe I went to exhibitions like that.

JOHN:

You're going to see one tonight.

ALMA:

Oh, no, I'm not.

JOHN:

That's what we came here for.

ALMA:

I didn't think such exhibitions were legal.

JOHN:

This is Moon Lake Casino where anything goes.

ALMA:

And you're a frequent patron?

JOHN:

I'd say constant.

ALMA:

Then I'm afraid you must be serious about giving up your medical career.

JOHN:

You bet I am! A doctor's life is walled in by sickness and misery and death.

ALMA:

May I be so presumptuous as to inquire what you'll do when you quit?

JOHN:

You may be so presumptuous as to inquire.

ALMA:

But you won't tell me?

JOHN:

I haven't made up my mind, but I've been thinking of South America lately.

ALMA [*sadly*]:

Oh . . .

JOHN:

I've heard that cantinas are lots more fun than saloons, and senoritas are caviar among females.

71

ALMA:
Dorothy Sykes' brother went to South America and was never heard of again. It takes a strong character to survive in the tropics. Otherwise it's a quagmire.

JOHN:
You think my character's weak?

ALMA:
I think you're confused, just awfully, awfully confused, as confused as I am—but in a different way. . . .

JOHN [*stretching out his legs*]:
Hee-haw, ho-hum.

ALMA:
You used to say that as a child—to signify your disgust!

JOHN [*grinning*]:
Did I?

ALMA [*sharply*]:
Don't sit like that!

JOHN:
Why not?

ALMA:
You look so indolent and worthless.

JOHN:
Maybe I am.

ALMA:
If you must go somewhere, why don't you choose a place with a bracing climate?

JOHN:
Parts of South America are as cool as a cucumber.

ALMA:
I never knew that.

JOHN:

Well, now you do.

ALMA:

Those Latins all dream in the sun—and indulge their senses.

JOHN:

Well, it's yet to be proven that anyone on this earth is crowned with so much glory as the one that uses his senses to get all he can in the way of—satisfaction.

ALMA:

Self-satisfaction?

JOHN:

What other kind is there?

ALMA:

I will answer that question by asking you one. Have you ever seen, or looked at a picture, of a Gothic cathedral?

JOHN:

Gothic cathedrals? What about them?

ALMA:

How everything reaches up, how everything seems to be straining for something out of the reach of stone—or human —fingers? . . . The immense stained windows, the great arched doors that are five or six times the height of the tallest man—the vaulted ceiling and all the delicate spires— all reaching up to something beyond attainment! To me— well, that is the secret, the principle back of existence—the everlasting struggle and aspiration for more than our human limits have placed in our reach. . . . Who was that said that—oh, so beautiful thing!—"All of us are in the gutter, but some of us are looking at the stars!"

JOHN:

Mr. Oscar Wilde.

ALMA [*somewhat taken aback*]:
Well, regardless of who said it, it's still true. Some of us
are looking at the stars! [*She looks up raptly and places her
hand over his.*]

JOHN:
It's no fun holding hands with gloves on, Miss Alma.

ALMA:
That's easily remedied. I'll just take the gloves off. [*Music
is heard.*]

JOHN:
Christ! [*He rises abruptly and lights a cigarette.*] Rosa Gonzales is dancing in the Casino.

ALMA:
You *are* unhappy. You hate me for depriving you of the
company inside. Well, you'll escape by and by. You'll drive
me home and come back out by yourself. . . . I've only gone
out with three young men at all seriously, and with each
one there was a desert between us.

JOHN:
What do you mean by a desert?

ALMA:
Oh—wide, wide stretches of uninhabitable ground.

JOHN:
Maybe you made it that way by being stand-offish.

ALMA:
I made quite an effort with one or two of them.

JOHN:
What kind of an effort?

ALMA:
Oh, I—tried to entertain them the first few times. I would
play and sing for them in the Rectory parlor.

JOHN:

With your father in the next room and the door half open?

ALMA:

I don't think that was the trouble.

JOHN:

What was the trouble?

ALMA:

I—I didn't have my heart in it. [*She laughs uncertainly.*]
A silence would fall between us. You know, a silence?

JOHN:

Yes, I know a silence.

ALMA:

I'd try to talk and he'd try to talk and neither would make
a go of it.

JOHN:

The silence would fall?

ALMA:

Yes, the enormous silence.

JOHN:

Then you'd go back to the piano?

ALMA:

I'd twist my ring. Sometimes I twisted it so hard that the
band cut my finger! He'd glance at his watch and we'd
both know that the useless undertaking had come to a
close. . . .

JOHN:

You'd call it quits?

ALMA:

Quits is—what we'd call it. . . . One or two times I was
rather sorry about it.

JOHN:

But you didn't have your heart in it?

ALMA:

None of them really engaged my serious feelings.

JOHN:

You do have serious feelings—of that kind?

ALMA:

Doesn't everyone—sometimes?

JOHN:

Some women are cold. Some women are what is called frigid.

ALMA:

Do I give that impression?

JOHN:

Under the surface you have a lot of excitement, a great deal more than any other woman I have met. So much that you have to carry these sleeping pills with you. The question is why? [*He leans over and lifts her veil.*]

ALMA:

What are you doing that for?

JOHN:

So that I won't get your veil in my mouth when I kiss you.

ALMA [*faintly*]:

Do you want to do that?

JOHN [*gently*]:

Miss Alma. [*He takes her arms and draws her to her feet.*] Oh, Miss Alma, Miss Alma! [*He kisses her.*]

ALMA [*in a low, shaken voice*]:

Not "Miss" any more. Just Alma.

JOHN [*grinning gently*]:

"Miss" suits you better, Miss Alma. [*He kisses her again. She hesitantly touches his shoulders, but not quite to push him away. John speaks softly to her.*] Is it so hard to forget you're a preacher's daughter?

ALMA:
There is no reason for me to forget that I am a minister's daughter. A minister's daughter's no different from any other young lady who tries to remember that she *is* a lady.

JOHN:
This lady stuff, is that so important?

ALMA:
Not to the sort of girls that you may be used to bringing to Moon Lake Casino. But suppose that some day . . . [*She crosses out of the arbor and faces away from him.*] suppose that some day you—*married. . . .* The woman that you selected to be your wife, and not only your wife but—the mother of your children! [*She catches her breath at the thought.*] Wouldn't you want that woman to be a lady? Wouldn't you want her to be somebody that you, as her husband, and they as her precious children—could look up to with very deep respect? [*There is a pause.*]

JOHN:
There's other things between a man and a woman besides respect. Did you know that, Miss Alma?

ALMA:
Yes. . . .

JOHN:
There's such a thing as intimate relations.

ALMA:
Thank you for telling me that. So plainly.

JOHN:
It may strike you as unpleasant. But it does have a good

77

deal to do with—connubial felicity, as you'd call it. There are some women that just give in to a man as a sort of obligation imposed on them by the—cruelty of nature! [*He finishes his glass and pours another.*] And there you are.

ALMA:
There *I* am?

JOHN:
I'm speaking generally.

ALMA:
Oh.

[*Hoarse shouts go up from the Casino.*]

JOHN:
The cock-fight has started!

ALMA:
Since you have spoken so plainly, I'll speak plainly, too. There are some women who turn a possibly beautiful thing into something no better than the coupling of beasts!—but love is what you bring to it.

JOHN:
You're right about that.

ALMA:
Some people bring just their bodies. But there are some people, there are some women, John—who can bring their hearts to it, also—who can bring their souls to it!

JOHN [*derisively*]:
Souls again, huh?—those Gothic cathedrals you dream of!

[*There is another hoarse prolonged shout from the Casino.*]

Your name is Alma and Alma is Spanish for soul. Some time I'd like to show you a chart of the human anatomy that I have in the office. It shows what our insides are like, and maybe you can show me where the beautiful soul is located on the chart. [*He drains the wine bottle.*] Let's go watch the cock-fight.

ALMA:

No! [*There is a pause.*]

JOHN:

I know something else we could do. There are rooms above the Casino. . . .

ALMA [*her back stiffening*]:

I'd heard that you made suggestions like that to girls that you go out with, but I refused to believe such stories were true. What made you think I might be amenable to such a suggestion?

JOHN:

I counted your pulse in the office the night you ran out because you weren't able to sleep.

ALMA:

The night I was ill and went to your father for help.

JOHN:

It was me you went to.

ALMA:

It was your father, and you wouldn't call your father.

JOHN:

Fingers frozen stiff when I . . .

ALMA [*rising*]:

Oh! I want to go home. But I won't go with you. I will go in a taxi! [*She wheels about hysterically.*] Boy! Boy! Call a taxi!

JOHN:

I'll call one for you, Miss Alma.—Taxi! [*He goes out of the arbor.*]

ALMA [*wildly*]:
You're not a gentleman!

JOHN [*from the darkness*]:
Taxi!

ALMA:
You're not a gentleman!

[*As he disappears she makes a sound in her throat like a hurt animal. The light fades out of the arbor and comes up more distinctly on the stone angel of the fountain.*]

SCENE SEVEN

The sky and the southern constellations, almost impercep-
tibly moving with the earth's motion, appear on the great
cyclorama.

The Rectory interior is lighted first, disclosing Alma and
Roger Doremus seated on the green plush sofa under the
romantic landscape in its heavy gilt frame. On a tiny table
beside them is a cut glass pitcher of lemonade with cherries
and orange slices in it, like a little aquarium of tropical fish.
Roger is entertaining Alma with a collection of photographs
and postcards, mementoes of his mother's trip to the Orient.
He is enthusiastic about them and describes them in phrases
his mother must have assimilated from a sedulous study of
literature provided by Cook's Tours. Alma is less enthusi-
astic; she is preoccupied with the sounds of a wild party
going on next door at the doctor's home. At present there is
Mexican music with shouts and stamping.

Only the immediate area of the sofa is clearly lighted; the
fountain is faintly etched in light and the night sky walls
the interior.

ROGER:
And this is Ceylon, The Pearl of the Orient!

ALMA:
And who is this fat young lady?

ROGER:
That is Mother in a hunting costume.

ALMA:
The hunting costume makes her figure seem bulky. What
was your mother hunting?

81

ROGER [*gaily*]:

Heaven knows what she was hunting! But she found Papa.

ALMA:

Oh, she met your father on this Oriental tour?

ROGER:

Ha-ha!—yes. . . . He was returning from India with dysentery and they met on the boat.

ALMA [*distastefully*]:

Oh . . .

ROGER:

And here she is on top of a ruined temple!

ALMA:

How did she get up there?

ROGER:

Climbed up, I suppose.

ALMA:

What an active woman.

ROGER:

Oh, yes, active—is no word for it! Here she is on an elephant's back in Burma.

ALMA:

Ah!

ROGER:

You're looking at it upside down, Miss Alma!

ALMA:

Deliberately—to tease you. [*The doorbell rings.*] Perhaps that's your mother coming to fetch you home.

ROGER:

It's only ten-fifteen. I never leave till ten-thirty.

[*Mrs. Bassett comes in.*]

82

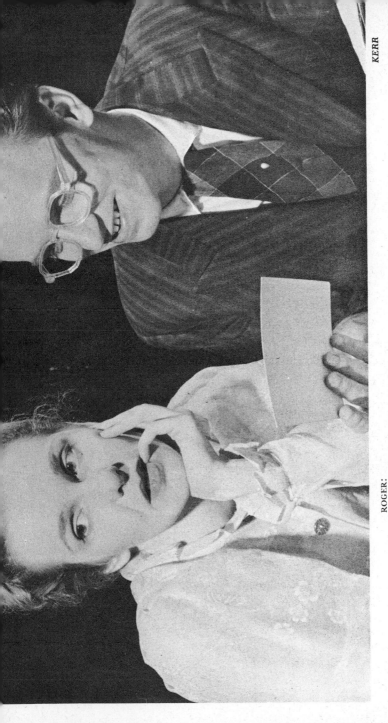

KERR

ROGER:
This is Mother in a hunting Costume.

ALMA:
(disinterested) What was your Mother hunting?

ROGER:
Heaven knows what she was hunting! But she found Papa.

ALMA:

Mrs. Bassett!

MRS. BASSETT:

I was just wondering who I could turn to when I saw the Rectory light and I thought to myself, Grace Bassett, you trot yourself right over there and talk to Mr. Winemiller!

ALMA:

Father has retired.

MRS. BASSETT:

Oh, what a pity. [She sees Roger.] Hello, Roger! . . . I saw that fall your mother took this morning. I saw her come skipping out of the Delta Planters' Bank and I thought to myself, now isn't that remarkable, a woman of her age and weight so light on her feet? And just at that very moment— *down she went!* I swear to goodness I thought she had broken her hip! Was she bruised much?

ROGER:

Just shaken up, Mrs. Bassett.

MRS. BASSETT:

Oh, how lucky! She certainly must be made out of India rubber! [*She turns to Alma.*] Alma—Alma, if it is not too late for human intervention, your father's the one right person to call up old Dr. Buchanan at the fever clinic at Lyon and let him know!

ALMA:

About—what?

MRS. BASSETT:

You must be stone-deaf if you haven't noticed what's been going on next door since the old doctor left to fight the epidemic. One continual orgy! Well, not five minutes ago a friend of mine who works at the County Courthouse called to inform me that young Dr. John and Rosa Gonzales have taken a license out and are going to be married tomorrow!

ALMA:

Are you—quite certain?

MRS. BASSETT:

Certain? I'm always certain before I speak!

ALMA:

Why would he—do such a thing?

MRS. BASSETT:

August madness! They say it has something to do with the falling stars. Of course it might also have something to do with the fact that he lost two or three thousand dollars at the Casino which he can't pay except by giving himself to Gonzales' daughter. [*She turns to Alma.*] Alma, what are you doing with that picture puzzle?

ALMA [*with a faint, hysterical laugh*]:

The pieces don't fit!

MRS. BASSETT [*to Roger*]:

I shouldn't have opened my mouth.

ALMA:

Will both of you please go!

[*Roger goes out.*]

MRS. BASSETT:

I knew this was going to upset you. Good night, Alma. [*She leaves. Alma suddenly springs up and seizes the telephone.*]

ALMA:

Long distance. . . . Please get me the fever clinic at Lyon. . . . I want to speak to Dr. Buchanan.

[*The light in the Rectory dims out and light comes on in the doctor's office. Rosa's voice is heard calling.*]

ROSA:

Johnny!

[*The offstage calling of John's name is used throughout the play as a cue for theme music.*

[*John enters the office interior. He is dressed, as always, in a white linen suit. His face has a look of satiety and confusion. He throws himself down in a swivel chair at the desk.*

[*Rosa Gonzales comes in. She is dressed in a Flamenco costume and has been dancing. She crosses and stands before the anatomy chart and clicks her castanets to catch his attention, but he remains looking up at the roofless dark. She approaches him.*]

ROSA:

You have blood on your face!

JOHN:

You bit my ear.

ROSA:

Ohhh . . . [*She approaches him with exaggerated concern.*]

JOHN:

You never make love without scratching or biting or something. Whenever I leave you I have a little blood on me. Why is that?

ROSA:

Because I know I can't hold you.

JOHN:

I think you're doing a pretty good job of it. Better than anyone else. Tomorrow we leave here together and Father or somebody else can tell old Mrs. Arbuckle her eighty-five years are enough and she's got to go now on the wings of carcinoma. Dance, Rosa! [*Accordion music is heard. She performs a slow and joyless dance around his chair. John continues while she dances.*] Tomorrow we leave here together. We sail out of Galveston, don't we?

ROSA:

You say it but I don't believe it.

JOHN:

I have the tickets.

ROSA:

Two pieces of paper that you can tear in two.

JOHN:

We'll go all right, and live on fat remittances from your Papa! Ha-ha!

ROSA:

Ha-ha-ha!

JOHN:

Not long ago the idea would have disgusted me, but not now. [*He catches her by the wrist.*] Rosa! Rosa Gonzales! Did anyone ever slide downhill as fast as I have this summer? Ha-ha! Like a greased pig. And yet every evening I put on a clean white suit. I have a dozen. Six in the closet and six in the wash. And there isn't a sign of depravity in my face. And yet all summer I've sat around here like *this,* remembering last night, anticipating the next one! The trouble with me is, I should have been *castrated!* [*He flings his wine glass at the anatomy chart. She stops dancing.*] Dance, Rosa! Why don't you dance? [*Rosa shakes her head dumbly.*] What is the matter, Rosa? Why don't you go on dancing? [*The accordion continues; he thrusts her arm savagely over her head in the Flamenco position.*]

ROSA [*suddenly weeping*]:

I can't dance any more! [*She throws herself to the floor, pressing her weeping face to his knees. The voice of her father is heard, bellowing, in the next room.*]

GONZALES:
The sky is the limit!

[*John is sobered.*]

JOHN:
Why does your father want me for a son-in-law?

ROSA [*sobbing*]:
I want you—I, I want you!

JOHN [*raising her from the floor*]:
Why do you?

ROSA [*clinging to him*]:
Maybe because—I was born in Piedras Negras, and grew up in a one room house with a dirt floor, and all of us had to sleep in that one room, five Mexicans and three geese and a little game-cock named Pepe! Ha-ha! [*She laughs hysterically.*] Pepe was a good fighter! That's how Papa began to make money, winning bets on Pepe! Ha-ha! We all slept in the one room. And in the night, I would hear the love-making. Papa would grunt like a pig to show his passion. I thought to myself, how dirty it was, love-making, and how dirty it was to be Mexicans and all have to sleep in one room with a dirt floor and not smell good because there was not any bathtub! [*The accordion continues.*]

JOHN:
What has that got to do with . . . ?

ROSA:
Me wanting you? You're tall! You smell good! And, oh, I'm so glad that you never grunt like a pig to show your passion! [*She embraces him convulsively.*] Ah, but *quien*

sabe! Something might happen tonight, and I'll wind up with some dark little friend of Papa's.

GONZALES [*imperiously*]:
Rosa! Rosa!

ROSA:
Si, si, Papa, aqui estoy!

GONZALES [*entering unsteadily*]:
The gold beads . . . [*He fingers a necklace of gold beads that Rosa is wearing.*] Johnny . . . [*He staggers up to John and catches him in a drunken embrace.*] Listen! When my girl Rosa was little she see a string a gold bead and she want those gold bead so bad that she cry all night for it. I don' have money to buy a string a gold bead so next day I go for a ride up to Eagle Pass and I walk in a dry good store and I say to the man: "Please give me a string a gold bead." He say: "Show me the money," and I say: "Here is the money!" And I reach down to my belt and I pull out—not the money—but this! [*He pulls out a revolver.*] Now—now I have money, but I still have this! [*laughing*] She got the gold bead. Anything that she want I get for her with this [*He pulls out a roll of bills.*] or this! [*He waves the revolver.*]

JOHN [*pushing Gonzales away*]:
Keep your stinking breath out of my face, Gonzales!

ROSA:
Dejalo, dejalo, Papa!

GONZALES [*moving unsteadily to the couch, with Rosa supporting him*]:
Le doy la tierra y si la tierra no basta—le doy el cielo! [*He collapses onto the couch.*] The sky is the limit!

ROSA [*to John*]:
Let him stay there. Come on back to the party.

My head's on fire—I will go in a minute but first I want you to put your hands on my face . . . Eternity and Miss Alma have such cool hands.

[*Rosa leaves the room. John goes over to the window facing the Rectory and looks across. The light comes up in the Rectory living room as Alma enters, dressed in a robe. She goes to the window and looks across at the doctor's house. As Alma and John stand at the windows looking toward each other through the darkness music is heard. Slowly, as if drawn by the music, John walks out of his house and crosses over to the Rectory. Alma remains motionless at the window until John enters the room, behind her. The music dies away and there is a murmur of wind. She slowly turns to face John.*]

JOHN:

I took the open door for an invitation. The Gulf wind is blowing tonight . . . cools things off a little. But my head's on fire. . . . [*Alma says nothing. John moves a few steps toward her.*] The silence? [*Alma sinks onto the love seat, closing her eyes.*] Yes, the enormous silence. [*He goes over to her.*] I will go in a minute, but first I want you to put your hands on my face. . . . [*He crouches beside her.*] Eternity and Miss Alma have such cool hands. [*He buries his face in her lap. The attitude suggests a stone Pietà. Alma's eyes remain closed.*]

[*On the other side of the stage Dr. Buchanan enters his house and the light builds a little as he looks around in the door of his office. The love theme music fades out and the Mexican music comes up strongly, with a definitely ominous quality, as Rosa enters the office from the other side.*]

ROSA:

Johnny! [*She catches sight of Dr. Buchanan and checks herself in surprise.*] Oh! I thought you were Johnny! . . . But you are Johnny's father. . . . I'm Rosa Gonzales!

DR. BUCHANAN:

I know who you are. What's going on in my house?

ROSA [*nervously*]:

John's giving a party because we're leaving tomorrow. [*defiantly*] Yes! Together! I hope you like the idea, but if you don't, it don't matter, because *we* like the idea and my father likes the idea.

GONZALES [*drunkenly, sitting up on the couch*]:
The sky is the limit!

[*Dr. Buchanan slowly raises his silver-headed cane in a threatening gesture.*]

DR. BUCHANAN:

Get your—swine out of—my house! [*He strikes Gonzales with his cane.*]

GONZALES [*staggering up from the couch in pain and surprise*]:
Aieeeee!

ROSA [*breathlessly, backing against the chart of anatomy*]:
No! No, Papa!

DR. BUCHANAN [*striking at the chest of the bull-like man with his cane*]:
Get your swine out, I said! Get them out of my house!

[*He repeats the blow. The drunken Mexican roars with pain and surprise. He backs up and reaches under his coat.*]

ROSA [*wildly and despairingly*]:
No, no, no, no, no, no!

[*She covers her face against the chart of anatomy. A revolver is fired. There is a burst of light. The cane drops. The music stops short. Everything dims out but a spot of light on Rosa standing against the chart of anatomy with closed eyes and her face twisted like that of a tragic mask.*]

ROSA [*senselessly*]:
Aaaaaahhhhhh . . . Aaaaaahhhhhh . . .

[*The theme music is started faintly and light disappears from everything but the wings of the stone angel.*]

The doctor's office.

The stone angel is dimly visible above.

John is seated in a hunched position at the table. Alma enters with a coffee tray. The sounds of a prayer come through the inner door.

JOHN:

What is that mumbo-jumbo your father is spouting in there?

ALMA:

A prayer.

JOHN:

Tell him to quit. We don't want that worn-out magic.

ALMA:

You may not want it, but it's not a question of what you want any more. I've made you some coffee.

JOHN:

I don't want any.

ALMA:

Lean back and let me wash your face off, John. [*She presses a towel to the red marks on his face.*] It's such a fine face, a fine and sensitive face, a face that has power in it that shouldn't be wasted.

JOHN:

Never mind that. [*He pushes her hand away.*]

ALMA:

You have to go in to see him.

JOHN:

I couldn't. He wouldn't want me.

ALMA:

This happened because of his devotion to you.

JOHN:

It happened because some meddlesome Mattie called him back here tonight. Who was it did that?

ALMA:

I did.

JOHN:

It *was* you then!

ALMA:

I phoned him at the fever clinic in Lyon as soon as I learned what you were planning to do. I wired him to come here and stop it.

JOHN:

You brought him here to be shot.

ALMA:

You can't put the blame on anything but your weakness.

JOHN:

You call me weak?

ALMA:

Sometimes it takes a tragedy like this to make a weak person strong.

JOHN:

You—white-blooded spinster! You so right people, pious pompous mumblers, preachers and preacher's daughter, all muffled up in a lot of worn-out magic! And I was supposed to minister to your neurosis, give you tablets for sleeping and tonics to give you the strength to go on mumbling your worn-out mumbo-jumbo!

ALMA:

Call me whatever you want, but don't let your father hear your drunken shouting. [*She tries to break away from him.*]

JOHN:

Stay here! I want you to look at something. [*He turns her about.*] This chart of anatomy, look!

ALMA:

I've seen it before. [*She turns away.*]

JOHN:

You've never dared to look at it.

ALMA:

Why should I?

JOHN:

You're scared to.

ALMA:

You must be out of your senses.

JOHN:

You talk about weakness but can't even look at a picture of human insides.

ALMA:

They're not important.

JOHN:

That's your mistake. You think you're stuffed with rose-leaves. Turn around and look at it, it may do you good!

ALMA:

How can you behave like this with your father dying and you so . . .

JOHN:

Hold still!

ALMA:
. . . so much to blame for it!

JOHN:
No more than you are!

ALMA:
At least for this little while . . .

JOHN:
Look here!

ALMA:
. . you could feel some shame!

JOHN [*with crazy, grinning intensity*]:
Now listen here to the anatomy lecture! This upper story's
the brain which is hungry for something called truth and
doesn't get much but keeps on feeling hungry! This middle's the belly which is hungry for food. This part down
here is the sex which is hungry for love because it is sometimes lonesome. I've fed all three, as much of all three as
I could or as much as I wanted— You've fed none—nothing.
Well—maybe your belly a little—watery subsistence— But
love or truth, nothing but—nothing but hand-me-down
notions!—attitudes!—poses! [*He releases her.*] Now you
can go. The anatomy lecture is over.

ALMA:
So that is your high conception of human desires. What you
have here is not the anatomy of a beast, but a man. And I
—I reject your opinion of where love is, and the kind of
truth you believe the brain to be seeking!—There is something not shown on the chart.

JOHN:
You mean the part that Alma is Spanish for, do you?

ALMA:
Yes, that's not shown on the anatomy chart! But it's there,

just the same, yes, there! Somewhere, not seen, but there. And it's *that* that I loved you with—that! Not what you mention!—Yes, did love you with, John, did nearly *die* of when you hurt me! [*He turns slowly to her and speaks gently.*]

JOHN:
I wouldn't have made love to you.

ALMA [*uncomprehendingly*]:
What?

JOHN:
The night at the Casino—I wouldn't have made love to you. Even if you had consented to go upstairs. I couldn't have made love to you. [*She stares at him as if anticipating some unbearable hurt.*] Yes, yes! Isn't that funny? I'm more afraid of your soul than you're afraid of my body. You'd have been as safe as the angel of the fountain—because I wouldn't feel *decent* enough to touch you. . . .

[*Mr. Winemiller comes in.*]

MR. WINEMILLER:
He's resting more easily now.

ALMA:
Oh . . . [*She nods her head. John reaches for his coffee cup.*] It's cold. I'll heat it.

JOHN:
It's all right.

MR. WINEMILLER:
Alma, Dr. John wants you.

ALMA:
I . . .

MR. WINEMILLER:
He asked if you would sing for him.

ALMA:
I—couldn't—now.

JOHN:
Go in and sing to him, Miss Alma!

[*Mr. Winemiller withdraws through the outer door. Alma looks back at John hunched over the coffee cup. He doesn't return her look. She passes into the blurred orange space beyond the inner door, leaving it slightly open. After a few minutes her voice rises softly within, singing. John suddenly rises. He crosses to the door, shoves it slowly open and enters.*]

JOHN [*softly and with deep tenderness*]:
Father?

[*The light dims out in the house, but lingers on the stone angel.*]

SCENE NINE

The cyclorama is the faint blue of a late afternoon in autumn. There is band-music—a Sousa march, in the distance. As it grows somewhat louder, Alma enters the Rectory interior in a dressing gown and with her hair hanging loose. She looks as if she had been through a long illness, the intensity drained, her pale face listless. She crosses to the window frame but the parade is not in sight so she returns weakly to the sofa and sits down closing her eyes with exhaustion.

The Rev. and Mrs. Winemiller enter the outer door frame of the Rectory, a grotesque-looking couple. Mrs. Winemiller has on her plumed hat, at a rakish angle, and a brilliant scarf about her throat. Her face wears a roguish smile that suggests a musical comedy pirate. One hand holds the minister's arm and with the other she is holding an ice cream cone.

MR. WINEMILLER:

Now you may let go of my arm, if you please! She was on her worst behavior. Stopped in front of the White Star Pharmacy on Front Street and stood there like a mule; wouldn't budge till I bought her an ice cream cone. I had it wrapped in tissue paper because she had promised me that she wouldn't eat it until we got home. The moment I gave it to her she tore off the paper and walked home licking it every step of the way!—just—just to humiliate me! [*Mrs. Winemiller offers him the half-eaten cone, saying "Lick?"*]

MR. WINEMILLER:

No, thank you!

ALMA:

Now, now, children.

[*Mr. Winemiller's irritation shifts to Alma.*]

MR. WINEMILLER:

Alma! Why don't you get dressed? It hurts me to see you sitting around like this, day in, day out, like an invalid when there is nothing particularly wrong with you. I can't read your mind. You may have had some kind of disappointment, but you must not make it an excuse for acting as if the world had come to an end.

ALMA:

I have made the beds and washed the breakfast dishes and phoned the market and sent the laundry out and peeled the potatoes and shelled the peas and set the table for lunch. What more do you want?

MR. WINEMILLER [*sharply*]:

I want you to either get dressed or stay in your room. [*Alma rises indifferently, then her father speaks suddenly.*] At night you get dressed. Don't you? Yes, I heard you slipping out of the house at two in the morning. And that was not the first time.

ALMA:

I don't sleep well. Sometimes I have to get up and walk for a while before I am able to sleep.

MR. WINEMILLER:

What am I going to tell people who ask about you?

ALMA:

Tell them I've changed and you're waiting to see in what way.

[*The band music becomes a little louder.*]

MR. WINEMILLER:
Are you going to stay like this indefinitely?

ALMA:
Not indefinitely, but you may wish that I had.

MR. WINEMILLER:
Stop twisting that ring! Whenever I look at you you're twisting that ring. Give me that ring! I'm going to take that ring off your finger! [*He catches her wrist. She breaks roughly away from him.*]

MRS. WINEMILLER [*joyfully*]:
Fight! Fight!

MR. WINEMILLER:
Oh, I give up!

ALMA:
That's better. [*She suddenly crosses to the window as the band music gets louder.*] Is there a parade in town?

MRS. WINEMILLER:
Ha-ha—yes! They met him at the station with a great big silver loving-cup!

ALMA:
Who? Who did they . . . ?

MRS. WINEMILLER:
That boy next door, the one you watched all the time!

ALMA:
Is that true, Father?

MR. WINEMILLER [*unfolding his newspaper*]:
Haven't you looked at the papers?

ALMA:
No, not lately.

MR. WINEMILLER [*wiping his eyeglasses*]:
These people are grasshoppers, just as likely to jump one

way as another. He's finished the work his father started, stamped out the fever and gotten all of the glory. Well, that's how it is in this world. Years of devotion and sacrifice are overlooked an' forgotten while someone young an' lucky walks off with the honors!

[*Alma has crossed slowly to the window. The sun brightens and falls in a shaft through the frame.*]

ALMA [*suddenly crying out*]:
There he is! [*She staggers away from the window. There is a roll of drums and then silence. Alma now speaks faintly.*] What . . . happened? Something . . . struck me! [*Mr. Winemiller catches her arm to support her.*]

MR. WINEMILLER:
Alma . . . I'll call a doctor.

ALMA:
No, no, don't. Don't call anybody to help me. I want to die!

[*She collapses on the sofa.*]

[*The band strikes up again and recedes down the street. The Rectory interior dims out. Then the light is brought up in the doctor's office. John enters, with his loving-cup. He is sprucely dressed and his whole manner suggests a new-found responsibility. While he is setting the award on the table, removing his coat and starched collar, Nellie Ewell appears in the door behind him. She stands by the anatomy chart and watches him until he discovers her presence. Nellie has abruptly grown up, and wears very adult clothes, but has lost none of her childish impudence and brightness. John gives a startled whistle as he sees her. Nellie giggles.*]

JOHN:
High heels, feathers . . . and paint!

NELLIE:
Not paint!

JOHN:
Natural color?

NELLIE:
Excitement.

JOHN:
Over what?

NELLIE:
Everything! You! You here! Didn't you see me at the depot? I shouted and waved my arm off! I'm home for Thanksgiving.

JOHN:
From where?

NELLIE:
Sophie Newcomb's. [*He remains staring at her, unbelieving. At last she draws a book from under her arm.*] Here is that nasty book you gave me last summer when I was pretending such ignorance of things!

JOHN:
Only pretending?

NELLIE:
Yes. [*He ignores the book. She tosses it on the table.*] ... Well? [*John laughs uneasily and sits on the table.*] Shall I go now, or will you look at my tongue? [*She crosses to him, sticking out her tongue.*]

JOHN:
Red as a berry!

NELLIE:
Peppermint drops! Will you have one? [*She holds out a sack.*]

JOHN:

Thanks. [*Nellie giggles as he takes one.*] What's the joke, Nellie?

NELLIE:

They make your mouth so sweet!

JOHN:

So?

NELLIE:

I always take one when I hope to be kissed.

JOHN [*after a pause*]:

Suppose I took you up on that?

NELLIE:

I'm not scared. Are you?

[*He gives her a quick kiss. She clings to him, raising her hand to press his head against her own. He breaks free after a moment and turns the light back on.*]

JOHN [*considerably impressed*]:

Where did you learn such tricks?

NELLIE:

I've been away to school. But they didn't teach me to love.

JOHN:

Who are you to be using that long word?

NELLIE:

That isn't a long word!

JOHN:

No?[*He turns away from her.*] Run along Nellie before we get into trouble.

NELLIE:

Who's afraid of trouble, you or me?

JOHN:

I am. Run along! Hear me?

NELLIE:

Oh, I'll go. But I'll be back for Christmas!

[*She laughs and runs out. He whistles and wipes his fore-head with a handkerchief.*]

SCENE TEN

An afternoon in December. At the fountain in the park. It is very windy.

Alma enters. She seems to move with an effort against the wind. She sinks down on the bench.

A widow with a flowing black veil passes across the stage and pauses by Alma's bench. It is Mrs. Bassett.

MRS. BASSETT:
Hello Alma.

ALMA:
Good afternoon, Mrs. Bassett.

MRS. BASSETT:
Such wind, such wind!

ALMA:
Yes, it nearly swept me off my feet. I had to sit down to catch my breath for a moment.

MRS. BASSETT:
I wouldn't sit too long if I were you.

ALMA:
No, not long.

MRS. BASSETT:
It's good to see you out again after your illness.

ALMA:
Thank you.

MRS. BASSETT:
Our poor little group broke up after you dropped out.

ALMA [*insincerely*]:
What a pity.

MRS. BASSETT:

You should have come to the last meeting.

ALMA:

Why, what happened?

MRS. BASSETT:

Vernon read his verse play!

ALMA:

Ah, how was it received?

MRS. BASSETT:

Maliciously, spitefully and vindictively torn to pieces, the way children tear the wings of butterflies. I think next Spring we might reorganize. [*She throws up her black-gloved hands in a deploring gesture.*]

[*Nellie Ewell appears. She is dressed very fashionably and carrying a fancy basket of Christmas packages.*]

NELLIE:

Miss Alma!

MRS. BASSETT [*rushing off*]:

Goodbye!

NELLIE:

Oh, there you are!

ALMA:

Why Nellie . . . Nellie Ewell!

NELLIE:

I was by the Rectory. Just popped in for a second; the holidays are so short that every minute is precious. They told me you'd gone to the park.

ALMA:

This is the first walk I've taken in quite a while.

NELLIE:

You've been ill!

ALMA:

Not ill, just not very well. How you've grown up, Nellie.

NELLIE:

It's just my clothes. Since I went off to Sophie Newcombe I've picked out my own clothes, Miss Alma. When Mother had jurisdiction over my wardrobe, she tried to keep me looking like a child!

ALMA:

Your voice is grown-up, too.

NELLIE:

They're teaching me diction, Miss Alma. I'm learning to talk like you, long A's and everything, such as "cahn't" and "bahth" and "lahf" instead of "laugh." Yesterday I slipped. I said I "lahfed and lahfed till I nearly died laughing." Johnny was so amused at me!

ALMA:

Johnny?

NELLIE:

Your nextdoor neighbor!

ALMA:

Oh! I'm sure it must be a very fashionable school.

NELLIE:

Oh yes, they're preparing us to be young ladies in society. What a pity there's no society here to be a young lady in . . . at least not for me, with Mother's reputation!

ALMA:

You'll find other fields to conquer.

NELLIE:

What's this I hear about *you?*

ALMA:

I have no idea, Nellie.

NELLIE:

That you've quit teaching singing and gone into retirement.

ALMA:

Naturally I had to stop teaching while I was ill and as for retiring from the world . . . it's more a case of the world retiring from me.

NELLIE:

I know somebody whose feelings you've hurt badly.

ALMA:

Why, who could that be, Nellie?

NELLIE:

Somebody who regards you as an angel!

ALMA:

I can't think who might hold me in such esteem.

NELLIE:

Somebody who says that you refused to see him.

ALMA:

I saw nobody. For several months. The long summer wore me out so.

NELLIE:

Well, anyhow, I'm going to give you your present. [*She hands her a small package from the basket.*]

ALMA:

Nellie, you shouldn't have given me anything.

NELLIE:

I'd like to know why not!

ALMA:

I didn't expect it.

NELLIE:

After the trouble you took with my horrible voice?

ALMA:

It's very sweet of you, Nellie.

NELLIE:

Open it!

ALMA:

Now?

NELLIE:

Why, sure.

ALMA:

It's so prettily wrapped I hate to undo it.

NELLIE:

I love to wrap presents and since it was for you, I did a specially dainty job of it.

ALMA [*winding the ribbon about her fingers*]:

I'm going to save this ribbon. I'm going to keep this lovely paper too, with the silver stars on it. And the sprig of holly . . .

NELLIE:

Let me pin it on your jacket, Alma.

ALMA:

Yes, do. I hardly realized that Christmas was coming. . . . [*She unfolds the paper, revealing a lace handkerchief and a card.*] What an exquisite handkerchief.

NELLIE:

I hate to give people handkerchiefs, it's so unimaginative.

ALMA:

I love to get them.

NELLIE:

It comes from Maison Blanche!

ALMA:

Oh, does it really?

NELLIE:

Smell it!

ALMA:

Sachet *Roses!* Well, I'm just more touched and pleased than I can possibly tell you!

NELLIE:

The card!

ALMA:

Card?

NELLIE:

You dropped it. [*She snatches up the card and hands it to Alma.*]

ALMA:

Oh, how clumsy of me! Thank you, Nellie. "Joyeux Noel ... to Alma ... from Nellie and ... [*She looks up slowly.*] John?"

NELLIE:

He helped me wrap presents last night and when we came to yours we started talking about you. Your ears must have burned!

[*The wind blows loudly. Alma bends stiffly forward.*]

ALMA:

You mean you—spoke well of me?

NELLIE:

"Well of"! We raved, simply raved! Oh, he told me the influence you'd had on him!

ALMA:

Influence?

NELLIE:

He told me about the wonderful talks he'd had with you

last summer when he was so mixed up and how you inspired him and you more than anyone else was responsible for his pulling himself together, after his father was killed, and he told me about . . . [*Alma rises stiffly from the bench.*] Where are you going, Miss Alma?

ALMA:
To drink at the fountain.

NELLIE:
He told me about how you came in the house that night like an angel of mercy!

ALMA [*laughing harshly by the fountain*]:
This is the only angel in Glorious Hill. [*She bends to drink.*] Her body is stone and her blood is mineral water.

[*The wind is louder.*]

NELLIE:
How penetrating the wind is!

ALMA:
I'm going home, Nellie. You run along and deliver your presents now. . . . [*She starts away.*]

NELLIE:
But wait till I've told you the wonderfullest thing I . . .

ALMA:
I'm going home now. Goodbye.

NELLIE:
Oh— Goodbye, Miss Alma.

[*She snatches up her festive basket and rushes in the other direction with a shrill giggle as the wind pulls at her skirts. The lights dim out.*]

SCENE ELEVEN

An hour later. In John's office.

The interior is framed by the traceries of Victorian architecture and there is one irregular section of wall supporting the anatomy chart. Otherwise the stage is open to the cyclorama.

In the background mellow golden light touches the vane of a steeple (a gilded weathercock). Also the wings of the stone angel. A singing wind rises and falls throughout scene.

John is seated at a white enameled table examining a slide through a microscope.

[*A bell tolls the hour of five as Alma comes hesitantly in. She, wears a russet suit and a matching hat with a plume. The light changes, the sun disappearing behind a cloud, fading from the steeple and the stone angel till the bell stops tolling. Then it brightens again.*]

ALMA:
No greetings? No greetings at all?

JOHN:
Hello, Miss Alma.

ALMA [*speaking with animation to control her panic*]:
How white it is here, such glacial brilliance! [*She covers her eyes, laughing.*]

JOHN:
New equipment. ;

ALMA:
Everything new but the chart.

JOHN:

The human anatomy's always the same old thing.

ALMA:

And such a tiresome one! I've been plagued with sore throats.

JOHN:

Everyone has here lately. These Southern homes are all improperly heated. Open grates aren't enough.

ALMA:

They burn the front of you while your back is freezing!

JOHN:

Then you go into another room and get chilled off.

ALMA:

Yes, yes, chilled to the bone.

JOHN:

But it never gets quite cold enough to convince the damn fools that a furnace is necessary so they go on building without them.

[*There is the sound of wind.*]

ALMA:

Such a strange afternoon.

JOHN:

Is it? I haven't been out.

ALMA:

The Gulf wind is blowing big, white—what do they call them? cumulus?—clouds over! Ha-ha! It seemed determined to take the plume off my hat, like that fox terrier we had once named Jacob, snatched the plume off a hat and dashed around and around the back yard with it like a trophy!

JOHN:

I remember Jacob. What happened to him?

ALMA:

Oh, Jacob. Jacob was such a mischievous thief. We had to send him out to some friends in the country. Yes, he ended his days as—a country squire! The tales of his exploits . . .

JOHN:

Sit down, Miss Alma.

ALMA:

If I'm disturbing you . . . ?

JOHN:

No—I called the Rectory when I heard you were sick. Your father told me you wouldn't see a doctor.

ALMA:

I needed a rest, that was all. . . . You were out of town mostly. . . .

JOHN:

I was mostly in Lyon, finishing up Dad's work in the fever clinic.

ALMA:

Covering yourself with sudden glory!

JOHN:

Redeeming myself with good works.

ALMA:

It's rather late to tell you how happy I am, and also how proud. I almost feel as your father might have felt—if . . . And—are you—happy now, John?

JOHN [*uncomfortably, not looking at her*]:

I've settled with life on fairly acceptable terms. Isn't that all a reasonable person can ask for?

114

ALMA:

He can ask for much more than that. He can ask for the coming true of his most improbable dreams.

JOHN:

It's best not to ask for too much.

ALMA:

I disagree with you. I say, ask for all, but be prepared to get nothing! [*She springs up and crosses to the window. She continues.*] No, I haven't been well. I've thought many times of something you told me last summer, that I have a *doppelganger*. I looked that up and I found that it means another person inside me, another self, and I don't know whether to thank you or not for making me conscious of it!—I haven't been well. . . . For a while I thought I was dying, that that was the change that was coming.

JOHN:

When did you have that feeling?

ALMA:

August. September. But now the Gulf wind has blown that feeling away like a cloud of smoke, and I know now I'm not dying, that it isn't going to turn out to be that simple. . . .

JOHN:

Have you been anxious about your heart again? [*He retreats to a professional manner and takes out a silver watch, putting his fingers on her wrist.*]

ALMA:

And now the stethoscope? [*He removes the stethoscope from the table and starts to loosen her jacket. She looks down at his bent head. Slowly, involuntarily, her gloved hands lift and descend on the crown of his head. He gets up awkwardly. She suddenly leans toward him and presses her mouth to his.*] Why don't you say something? Has the cat got your tongue?

JOHN:
Miss Alma, what can I say?

ALMA:
You've gone back to calling me "Miss Alma" again.

JOHN:
We never really got past that point with each other.

ALMA:
Oh, yes, we did. We were so close that we almost breathed together!

JOHN [*with embarrassment*]:
I didn't know that.

ALMA:
No? Well, I did, I knew it. [*Her hand touches his face tenderly.*] You shave more carefully now? You don't have those little razor cuts on your chin that you dusted with gardenia talcum. . . .

JOHN:
I shave more carefully now.

ALMA:
So that explains it! [*Her fingers remain on his face, moving gently up and down it like a blind person reading Braille. He is intensely embarrassed and gently removes her hands from him.*] Is it—impossible now?

JOHN:
I don't think I know what you mean.

ALMA:
You know what I mean, all right! So be honest with me. One time I said "no" to something. You may remember the time, and all that demented howling from the cock-fight?

But now I have changed my mind, or the girl who said
"no," she doesn't exist any more, she died last summer
—suffocated in smoke from something on fire inside
her. No, she doesn't live now, but she left me her
ring— You see? This one you admired, the topaz ring set
in pearls. . . . And she said to me when she slipped this
ring on my finger—"Remember I died empty-handed, and
so make sure that your hands have *something in them!*"
[*She drops her gloves. She clasps his head again in her
hands.*] I said, "But what about pride?"—She said, "Forget
about pride whenever it stands between you and what you
must have!" [*He takes hold of her wrists.*] And then I said,
"But what if he doesn't want me?" I don't know what she
said then. I'm not sure whether she said anything or not—
her lips stopped moving—yes, I think she stopped breath-
ing! [*He gently removes her craving hands from his face.*]
No? [*He shakes his head in dumb suffering.*] Then the answer is "no"!

JOHN [*forcing himself to speak*]:
I have a respect for the truth, and I have a respect for you—
so I'd better speak honestly if you want me to speak. [*Alma
nods slightly.*] You've won the argument that we had between us.

ALMA:
What—argument?

JOHN:
The one about the chart.

ALMA:
Oh—the chart!

[*She turns from him and wanders across to the chart.
She gazes up at it with closed eyes, and her hands clasped
in front of her.*]

JOHN:

It shows that we're not a package of rose leaves, that every interior inch of us is taken up with something ugly and functional and no room seems to be left for anything else in there.

ALMA:

No...

JOHN:

But I've come around to your way of thinking, that something else is in there, an immaterial something—as thin as smoke—which all of those ugly machines combine to produce and that's their whole reason for being. It can't be seen so it can't be shown on the chart. But it's there, just the same, and knowing it's there—why, then the whole thing—this—this unfathomable experience of ours—takes on a new value, like some—some wildly romantic work in a laboratory! Don't you see?

[*The wind comes up very loud, almost like a choir of voices. Both of them turn slightly, Alma raising a hand to her plumed head as if she were outdoors.*]

ALMA:

Yes, I see! Now that you no longer want it to be otherwise you're willing to believe that a spiritual bond can exist between us two!

JOHN:

Can't you believe that I am sincere about it?

ALMA:

Maybe you are. But I don't want to be talked to like some incurably sick patient you have to comfort. [*A harsh and strong note comes into her voice.*] Oh, I suppose I am sick, one of those weak and divided people who slip like shadows among you solid strong ones. But sometimes, out of neces-

118

sity, we shadowy people take on a strength of our own. I have that now. You needn't try to deceive me.

JOHN:
I wasn't.

ALMA:
You needn't try to comfort me. I haven't come here on any but equal terms. You said, let's talk truthfully. Well, let's do! Unsparingly, truthfully, even shamelessly, then! It's no longer a secret that I love you. It never was. I loved you as long ago as the time I asked you to read the stone angel's name with your fingers. Yes, I remember the long afternoons of our childhood, when I had to stay indoors to practice my music—and heard your playmates calling you, "Johnny, Johnny!" How it went through me, just to hear your name called! And how I—rushed to the window to watch you jump the porch railing! I stood at a distance, halfway down the block, only to keep in sight of your torn red sweater, racing about the vacant lot you played in. Yes, it had begun that early, this affliction of love, and has never let go of me since, but kept on growing. I've lived next door to you all the days of my life, a weak and divided person who stood in adoring awe of your singleness, of your strength. And that is my story! Now I wish *you* would tell *me*—why didn't it happen between us? Why did I fail? Why did you come almost close enough—and no closer?

JOHN:
Whenever we've gotten together, the three or four times that we have . . .

ALMA:
As few as that?

JOHN:
It's only been three or four times that we've—come face to

face. And each of those times—we seemed to be trying to find something in each other without knowing what it was that we wanted to find. It wasn't a body hunger although— I acted as if I thought it might be the night I wasn't a gentleman—at the Casino—it wasn't the physical you that I really wanted!

ALMA:
I know, you've already . . .

JOHN:
You didn't have that to give me.

ALMA:
Not at that time.

JOHN:
You had something else to give.

ALMA:
What did I have?

[*John strikes a match. Unconsciously he holds his curved palm over the flame of the match to warm it. It is a long kitchen match and it makes a good flame. They both stare at it with a sorrowful understanding that is still perplexed. It is about to burn his fingers. She leans forward and blows it out, then she puts on her gloves.*]

JOHN:
You couldn't name it and I couldn't recognize it. I thought it was just a Puritanical ice that glittered like flame. But now I believe it *was* flame, mistaken for ice. I still don't understand it, but I know it was there, just as I know that your eyes and your voice are the two most beautiful things I've ever known—and also the warmest, although they don't seem to be set in your body at all. . . .

ALMA:

One time I said "no" to someone...but the girl who said
"no" doesn't exist anymore, she died last summer—suffocated
in smoke from something on fire inside her.

ALMA:

You talk as if my body had ceased to exist for you, John, in spite of the fact that you've just counted my pulse. Yes, that's it! You tried to avoid it, but you've told me plainly. The tables have turned, yes, the tables have turned with a vengeance! You've come around to my old way of thinking and I to yours like two people exchanging a call on each other at the same time, and each one finding the other one gone out, the door locked against him and no one to answer the bell! [*She laughs.*] I came here to tell you that being a gentleman, doesn't seem so important to me any more, but you're telling me I've got to remain a lady. [*She laughs rather violently.*] The tables have turned with a vengeance! —The air in here smells of ether— It's making me dizzy . . .

JOHN:

I'll open a window.

ALMA:

Please.

JOHN:

There now.

ALMA:

Thank you, that's better. Do you remember those little white tablets you gave me? I've used them all up and I'd like to have some more.

JOHN:

I'll write the prescription for you. [*He bends to write.*]

[*Nellie is in the waiting room. They hear her voice.*]

ALMA:

Someone is waiting in the waiting room, John. One of my vocal pupils. The youngest and prettiest one with the least gift for music. The one that you helped wrap up this handkerchief for me. [*She takes it out and touches her eyes with it.*]

[*The door opens, first a crack. Nellie peers in and giggles. Then she throws the door wide open with a peal of merry laughter. She has holly pinned on her jacket. She rushes up to John and hugs him with childish squeals.*]

NELLIE:
I've been all over town just shouting, shouting!

JOHN:
Shouting what?

NELLIE:
Glad tidings!

[*John looks at Alma over Nellie's shoulder.*]

JOHN:
I thought we weren't going to tell anyone for a while.

NELLIE:
I couldn't stop myself. [*She wheels about.*] Oh, Alma, has he told *you?*

ALMA [*quietly*]:
He didn't need to, Nellie. I guessed . . . from the Christmas card with your two names written on it!

[*Nellie rushes over to Alma and hugs her. Over Nellie's shoulder Alma looks at John. He makes a thwarted gesture as if he wanted to speak. She smiles desperately and shakes her head. She closes her eyes and bites her lips for a moment. Then she releases Nellie with a laugh of exaggerated gaiety.*]

NELLIE:
So Alma you were really the first to know!

ALMA:

I'm proud of that, Nellie.

NELLIE:

See on my finger! This was the present I couldn't tell you about!

ALMA:

Oh, what a lovely, lovely solitaire! But solitaire is such a wrong name for it. Solitaire means single and this means *two!* It's blinding, Nellie! Why it . . . hurts my eyes!

[*John catches Nellie's arm and pulls her to him. Almost violently Alma lifts her face; it is bathed in tears. She nods gratefully to John for releasing her from Nellie's attention. She picks up her gloves and purse.*]

JOHN:

Excuse her, Miss Alma. Nellie's still such a child.

ALMA [*with a breathless laugh*]:
I've got to run along now.

JOHN:

Don't leave your prescription.

ALMA:

Oh, yes, where's my prescription?

JOHN:

On the table.

ALMA:

I'll take it to the drug store right away!

[*Nellie struggles to free herself from John's embrace which keeps her from turning to Alma.*]

NELLIE:

Alma, don't go! Johnny, let go of me, Johnny! You're hugging me so tight I can't breathe!

123

ALMA:

Goodbye.

NELLIE:

Alma! Alma, you know you're going to sing at the wedding! The very first Sunday in Spring!—which will be Palm Sunday! "The Voice that Breathed o'er Eden."

[*Alma has closed the door. John shuts his eyes tight with a look of torment. He rains kisses on Nellie's forehead and throat and lips. The scene dims out with music.*]

SCENE TWELVE

In the park near the angel of the fountain. About dusk.

Alma enters the lighted area and goes slowly up to the fountain and bends to drink. Then she removes a small white package from her pocketbook and starts to unwrap it. While she is doing this, a Young Man comes along. He is dressed in a checked suit and a derby. He pauses by the bench. They glance at each other.

A train whistles in the distance. The Young Man clears his throat. The train whistle is repeated. The Young Man crosses toward the fountain, his eyes on Alma. She hesitates, with the unwrapped package in her hand. Then she crosses toward the bench and stands hesitantly in front of it. He stuffs his hands in his pockets and whistles. He glances with an effect of unconcern back over his shoulder.

Alma pushes her veil back with an uncertain gesture. His whistle dies out. He sways back and forth on his heels as the train whistles again. He suddenly turns to the fountain and bends to drink. Alma slips the package back into her purse. As the young man straightens up, she speaks in a barely audible voice.

ALMA:
The water—is—cool.

THE YOUNG MAN [*eagerly*]:
Did you say something?

ALMA:
I said, the water is cool.

125

THE YOUNG MAN:
Yes, it sure is, it's nice and cool!

ALMA:
It's always cool.

THE YOUNG MAN:
Is it?

ALMA:
Yes. Yes, even in summer. It comes from deep underground.

THE YOUNG MAN:
That's what keeps it cool.

ALMA:
Glorious Hill is famous for its artesian springs.

THE YOUNG MAN:
I didn't know that.

[*The Young Man jerkily removes his hands from his pockets. She gathers confidence before the awkwardness of his youth.*]

ALMA:
Are you a stranger in town?

THE YOUNG MAN:
I'm a traveling salesman.

ALMA:
Ah, you're a salesman who travels! [*She laughs gently.*] But you're younger than most of them are, and not so fat!

THE YOUNG MAN:
I'm just starting out. I travel for Red Goose shoes.

ALMA:
Ah! The Delt's your territory?

THE YOUNG MAN:
From the Peabody Lobby to Cat-Fish Row in Vicksburg.

[*Alma leans back and looks at him under half-closed lids, perhaps a little suggestively.*]

ALMA:
The life of a traveling salesman is interesting . . . but lonely.

THE YOUNG MAN:
You're right about that. Hotel bedrooms are lonely.

[*There is a pause. Far away the train whistles again.*]

ALMA:
All rooms are lonely where there is only one person. [*Her eyes fall shut.*]

THE YOUNG MAN [*gently*]:
You're tired, aren't you?

ALMA:
I? Tired? [*She starts to deny it; then laughs faintly and confesses the truth.*] Yes . . . a little. . . . But I shall rest now. I've just now taken one of my sleeping tablets.

THE YOUNG MAN:
So early?

ALMA:
Oh, it won't put me to sleep. It will just quiet my nerves.

THE YOUNG MAN:
What are you nervous about?

ALMA:
I won an argument this afternoon.

THE YOUNG MAN:
That's nothing to be nervous over. You ought to be nervous if you *lost* one.

ALMA:
It wasn't the argument that I wanted to win. . . .

127

THE YOUNG MAN:
Well, I'm nervous too.

ALMA:
What over?

THE YOUNG MAN:
It's my first job and I'm scared of not making good.

[*That mysteriously sudden intimacy that sometimes oc-curs between strangers more completely than old friends or lovers moves them both. Alma hands the package of tablets to him.*]

ALMA:
Then you must take one of my tablets.

THE YOUNG MAN:
Shall I?

ALMA:
Please take one!

THE YOUNG MAN:
Yes, I shall.

ALMA:
You'll be surprised how infinitely merciful they are. The prescription number is 96814. I think of it as the telephone number of God! [*They both laugh. He places one of the tablets on his tongue and crosses to the fountain to wash it down.*]

THE YOUNG MAN [*to the stone figure*]:
Thanks, angel. [*He gives her a little salute, and crosses back to Alma.*]

ALMA:
Life is full of little mercies like that, not *big* mercies but comfortable *little* mercies. And so we are able to keep on going. . . . [*She has leaned back with half-closed eyes.*]

THE YOUNG MAN [*returning*]:
You're falling asleep.

ALMA:
Oh no, I'm not. I'm just closing my eyes. You know what I feel like now? I feel like a water-lily.

THE YOUNG MAN:
A water-lily?

ALMA:
Yes, I feel like a water-lily on a Chinese lagoon. Won't you sit down? [*The Young Man does.*] My name is Alma. Spanish for soul! What's yours?

THE YOUNG MAN:
Ha-ha! Mine's Archie Kramer. Mucho gusto, as they say in Spain.

ALMA:
Usted habla Espanol, senor?

THE YOUNG MAN:
Un poquito! Usted habla Espanol, senorita?

ALMA:
Me tambien. Un poquito!

THE YOUNG MAN [*delightedly*]:
Ha . . . ha . . . ha! Sometimes un poquito is plenty! [*Alma laughs . . . in a different way than she has ever laughed before, a little wearily, but quite naturally. The Young Man leans toward her confidentially.*] What's there to do in this town after dark?

ALMA:
There's not much to do in this town after dark, but there are resorts on the lake that offer all kinds of after-dark entertainment. There's one called Moon Lake Casino. It's

under new management, now, but I don't suppose its character has changed.

THE YOUNG MAN:
What was its character?

ALMA:
Gay, very gay, Mr. Kramer. . . .

THE YOUNG MAN:
Then what in hell are we sitting here for? Vamonos!

ALMA:
Como no, senor!

THE YOUNG MAN:
Ha-ha-ha! [*He jumps up.*] I'll call a taxi. [*He goes off shouting "Taxi."*]

[*Alma rises from the bench. As she crosses to the fountain the grave mood of the play is reinstated with a phrase of music. She faces the stone angel and raises her gloved hand in a sort of valedictory salute. Then she turns slowly about toward the audience with her hand still raised in a gesture of wonder and finality as . . . the curtain falls.*]